RECLAIMING
THE MOSQUE

RECLAIMING THE MOSQUE

THE ROLE OF WOMEN IN ISLAM'S HOUSE OF WORSHIP

JASSER AUDA

CLARITAS
BOOKS

1 2 3 4 5 6 7 8 9 10

CLARITAS BOOKS

Bernard Street, Swansea, United Kingdom
Militias, California, United States

CLARITAS
BOOKS

© CLARITAS BOOKS 2017

CLARITAS BOOKS in association with Maqasid Institute

First Published in June 2017

© Cover photo Mosa'ab Elshamy
Dr. Heba Raouf teaching at Sultan Hassan Mosque, Cairo

Typeset in Minion Pro
Printed by Mega Printing in Turkey

Reclaiming the Mosque: The Role of Women in
Islam's House of Worship
By Jasser Auda

A CIP catalogue record for this book is available from the British Library

ISBN: 978-1-905837-40-3

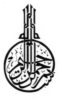

JASSER AUDA is the Chairman of the Maqasid Institute, a global think tank with educational and research projects. He is a Professor and Al-Shatibi Chair of Maqasid Studies at the International Peace College in South Africa and a Visiting Professor for the Study of Islam at Carleton University in Canada. Jasser Auda is a Member of the Executive Board of the Fiqh Council of North America, Member of the European Council for Fatwa and Research and Fellow of the Islamic Fiqh Academy of India. He was the Founding Director of the Maqasid Center in the Philosophy of Islamic Law in London; Founding Deputy Director of the Center for Islamic Legislation and Ethics in Doha; and a Professor at the University of Waterloo (Canada), Alexandria University (Egypt) and Qatar Faculty of Islamic Studies (Qatar). He has a PhD in the Philosophy of Islamic Law from University of Wales (UK) and a PhD in Systems Analysis from University of Waterloo (Canada). Early in his life, he memorised the Quran and studied Fiqh, Usul and Hadith in the study circles of Al-Azhar Mosque in Cairo. Dr Jasser has lectured on Islam, its law, spirituality and ethics in many countries across the world. He has written 25 books in Arabic and English, some of which have been translated into twenty five languages.

CONTENTS

~

CHAPTER 1

Why this book?

A few years ago, the British Channel 4 *Dispatches* programme aired an interesting episode about Muslim women in the UK. They investigated the role of Muslim women in London mosques and their contribution to their communities. To their shock, and my embarrassment as a viewer, it concluded that women have no role in most of the mosques they surveyed. This was due to the simple fact that women were not even "allowed" to enter them in the first place.

The female reporter, dressed in a conservative Muslim garment, attempted to enter dozens of mosques in London, on camera. She was told at the door, sometimes politely but oftentimes rudely that, "No women are allowed here," or found someone at the mosque's door pointing to a sign that read: "Brothers Only".

The documentary reported that about 800 London mosques are not open to women. Mosque leaders, who agreed to be interviewed, cited "limited space" as the main reason for this. When the reporter questioned, "But why aren't women allowed in the available space at any time? What is the role of the mosque anyway?" she received no reply.

This documentary undoubtedly caused damage to Islam's image in the UK and around the world. To me, it was a scandal, in all senses of the word. I remembered our late Sheikh Mohammed Al-Ghazali's words: "Islam has a very good case to make, but it has very bad lawyers!" His book, *Muslim Women Between Stagnant Traditions and Modern Innovations*,[1] includes dozens of examples of baseless cultural traditions that have negatively impacted Muslim women and their social role. In the introduction of the book, Sheikh Al-Ghazali cited the hadith of the female companion, Umm Waraqah, who used to lead men and women in congregational prayers in the mosque adjoined to her home.[2] He also cited other stories of the Prophet's female companions praying in the Prophet's Mosque, trading in their local and regional markets, teaching Quran and the prophetic traditions, giving charity, and even fighting in the battlefield alongside the Prophet (s) and his male companions. What a great difference between the status of women in the early days of Islam and today, I thought.

Over the past few years, many research articles, social media reports and television programmes have emerged, all with similar themes and findings, to speak out against the marginalisation of women in mosques around the world. One of the most well researched documentations on the topic was the American movie, *UnMosqued*.[3] The film was made based on research that involved hundreds of mosques and thousands of individuals in the United States. The two most alarming conclusions were: (1) mosque attendance in the US is significantly declining, despite the increase of numbers of Muslims; and (2) women in American mosques, where and when they are allowed to attend, are treated as "second class citizens".

In terms of statistics, *UnMosqued* reported very low numbers of attendance from women and children in American mosques, versus men. In terms of women's spaces, it was reported that two thirds of the mosques that allowed women in, used dividers or walls to partition their spaces, and that the number of dividers was actually increasing over the years. It was also noted that women's spaces were always of lower quality than men's spaces. "African American mosques" proved to be more inclusive to women than "Arab mosques", they said, and almost all mosques did not think that women's activities or programmes were a "top priority". Finally, researchers found out that the more women-friendly the mosque is, the more likely it is to provide community services, interfaith sessions, and involve children and youth.

Considering these developments, I was asked by some American sisters whether it is possible, from an Islamic jurisprudential point of view, to have their own all-women mosque and to hold congregational prayers including Friday prayers. My answer was that it is "permissible" to build such a mosque from a pure "schools of Islamic law" perspective. There are undisputed precedents from the Prophet's time when women led other women in the five daily prayers, except for the Friday prayer that includes a pre-prayer sermon. Therefore, I suggested that one of our sisters offer a sermon, but then to be on the safe side, pray four *rak'as* (units) for *dhuhr* (noon prayers) rather than the two usual *rak'as* for Friday prayer. That said, I added that just as the all-male mosques go against the general principles and *maqasid* (intents) of Islamic jurisprudence, including unity and cooperation of the community of believers, all-female mosques would as well.

To me, women's mosques are a temporary solution and a way to protest women's marginalisation in today's mosques, but in the longer term they would serve to divide our communities even further. Unfortunately, many mosques are already divided along racial lines, such as Arab, Turkish, Indian and Afro-American mosques, and along jurisprudential schools, such as Sunni, Shia, Hanafi, and Ibadhi mosques, and along political ideologies, such as Salafi, Ikhwan, Hizbul-Tahrir, and Sufi mosques. All of these divisions are forbidden innovations (*bid'ah*) in the faith. And here is yet another division: men's mosques and women's mosques.

We will see, from ample evidence throughout this book, that the Prophet's Mosque was for everyone: for the Arab, the African, the Persian, the Roman, for men, women, and children, and for Muslims and non-Muslims who wished to visit. This demonstrated the strength of the early Muslim community's "state of the union". Today it is likewise a measure of how weak this union has become.

The place and role of women in the mosques is in real crisis worldwide, not just in the UK and America. The status quo must change. This very central Islamic social and spiritual institution is missing half of the *ummah* where light, guidance, knowledge and true bonds of faith and kinship are nurtured. Further, we are giving the worst impression to non-Muslims, who are not to be blamed when they develop (mis)conceptions about Islam as a religion that does not welcome women and does not treat them with full dignity, justice, mercy and rights.

Therefore, I decided to research and write about the place and role of women in the mosque according to Islamic jurisprudence, as understood based on the original sources of Islam. The story of this book started with a research paper that I wrote for the 2015 Annual Regular Meeting of the European Council for Fatwa and Research (ECFR), of which I am a member. The meeting was held under the theme: "European Muslim Women and their Needs". Based on the paper, the Council made the following declaration:

- It is forbidden to prevent women from their right to visit the mosque.
- Muslim women must be encouraged to attend the mosque.
- The tradition of the Prophet (s), did not include barriers between men and women in the mosque.
- It is an obligation to protect women in the mosque from any mistreatment or harassment.
- A non-Muslim woman should be allowed to visit the mosque, with or without a headscarf, as long as she is dressed decently.
- A woman is allowed to stay in seclusion (*i'tikaf*) in the mosque and to visit others who are staying there.
- A woman can and may lecture to men and women in the mosque.
- A woman can and may participate in the mosque's management and all social activities.

Given the positive reactions that this declaration elicited, I decided to expand on the paper and publish it in the form of essays in Arabic and English,[4] on social media and in various newspapers, and to present its content in my Friday sermons and public lectures around the world.

These essays, sermons and lectures turned out to be quite popular, and have been translated in a number of languages and published in many forms.[5] The feedback that I have received ranges from expressions of relief in knowing that women do have an important role in the mosque, to expressions of concern at the "feminist tone" of the essays and the risk of encouraging "immorality", "modernism" and posing a "challenge to male leadership" in our mosques. We need, however, to go beyond emotional and uninformed reactions toward more concrete steps to improve the current predicament.

Then, I re-structured the material in the essays and lectures in the form of 20 questions, which comprise the 20 chapters of this book. I hope that the answers provided here address the unfounded concerns mentioned above, while embracing an authentic, rational, moral and moderate path in dealing with issues of women in the mosque and in Islamic jurisprudence in general.

Finally, wrong interpretations and distasteful opinions on the status of women in Islam contribute in a direct way to the plight of women everywhere today, and this is a serious problem that requires immediate attention and deep change. I am hoping that this book will be a part of that change, and will encourage others, men and women, to have the courage to speak up and make a difference.

A genuine revival and tangible contribution of the Muslim ummah to humanity will never materialise without the full participation and active engagement of Muslim women, not only in the mosque, but also in Islamic scholarship and Muslim affairs more broadly.

All praise is due to Allah, the Lord of the Worlds.

JASSER AUDA
Ottawa, Canada
Rabi' Al-Akhir 1438, January 2017

~

CHAPTER 2

How do we judge what is "Islamic"?

I was in Southeast Asia a couple of years ago, when a group of young Muslims enthusiastically invited me to watch the "first Islamic movie in history." I asked: What is "Islamic" about the movie? They said that they had a "Sharia Committee" which decided that the movie should have no women and no music. To get around the issue of female characters, male actors wore headscarves with their backs to the camera, they explained. The music, they said, was created without any musical instruments. I asked: "What about the storyline?" They said that the sayings are all from the Companions' dialogues – all authentic narrations, and the story is not important. I asked, "Do you have an audience?" They said that tickets had been sold out for the third run with each showing lasting a month. In the end, they could not even get me tickets to watch the movie.

Another time, I was in the Caribbean when I was invited to stay in a popular "Islamic hotel" on the beach. When I checked into my room, I found no windows – only four walls and a door! Later, the receptionist informed me that the Muslim owners of the hotel decided to design the whole hotel without windows in any room, despite its beachfront location, to provide full privacy to its guests. I was also assured that breakfast is "halal". It was interesting to see that breakfast was only fruits, eggs, bread, milk, and tea. When I saw that everything, to my surprise, was labelled "halal," I wondered how could eggs, milk or tea not be halal? And yet the hotel was fully occupied!

The above are two examples of successful "Islamic" and "halal" projects that have gained wide popularity. Unfortunately, they are quite representative of many things identified as "Islamic" and "halal" today. What made that movie "Islamic" in the minds of the "Sharia Committee" members was the absence of women and musical instruments, while the content of the story was irrelevant. The hotel was considered "Islamic" because of the "halal" labels on eggs and milk, and the absence of windows!

Without sounding too cynical, I believe that many "Islamic" labels today are given without justification. Many "Islamic banks" are part and parcel of the world's capitalistic, monopolistic and unfair economic system, yet they are "Islamic" because a "Sharia Committee" has labelled them as such. These committees, which by the way never have female members, often give "halal" stamps to financial transactions that do not qualify just because they meet certain superficial criteria of resemblance to historical financial dealings. The bigger picture, i.e. the Islamic moral values and philosophy at the macro-economic level, is irrelevant to them.

Many "Islamic slaughterhouses" are typical slaughterhouses, yet they are "Islamic" because they hire a Muslim to recite *bismillah* (in the name of Allah) every time an animal is slaughtered. In some cases, it is only a bismillah "sound bite" that is pre-recorded and repeated automatically on a computer in the room. There are no Islamic ethical standards for the treatment of the animals or birds, including watering, feeding and sheltering conditions. Last year, I refused to join one of those "Halal Committees" and I told them that a computer-generated sound does not make slaughtering "halal" or "Islamic".

Similarly, many "Islamic political parties" undertake politics as usual, in the same Machiavellian, divisive and corrupt ways. Yet, the labels "Islamic" and "Sharia-compliant" allow them to appeal unconditionally to some uninformed voters, or to play identity politics to win more power in elections. If the priorities of the "Islamic party" do not include the welfare of the people who are subject to their governance, and if they change nothing in the plight of the insecure, the hungry, the homeless, the economically vulnerable and the uneducated, then what does "Islamic" mean?

It is very important before dealing with any topic from an "Islamic" perspective, to define what we mean by the very term. The true reference to what is Islamic is nothing other than the Word of God, the original source and the founding document of Islam, the Quran, and the example or *Sunnah* of His Prophet (s), who was a living illustration of the Quran.

The question here, however, is *how* do we read the Quran and Sunnah? This is the essential question of methodology, and failing to address it adequately results in misguided opinions and incorrect decisions, like the ones mentioned above. Methodology, however, requires a separate and long discussion that is beyond the scope of this book.[6]

Nevertheless, for the purpose of this book, the following is a quick classification of three popular readings that do not fulfil the standards set by the Quran itself as to how it should be read and how we should deal with the Sunnah of the Prophet (s).

1. Partial readings: Allah warns us from "partitioning" the Quran and "believing in some of it while reject-ing some of it."[7] In the following chapters, we will discuss how some verses or hadith narrations are misread or misunderstood, because of the partial or narrow view with which they were approached. Some verses or narrations are read in isolation from other related and relevant verses and narrations, or without giving due consideration to the context of time or related circumstances. Hence, the outcome is interpretations that contradict the principles of Is-lam, even though they could still be called "Islamic." Another partial reading is to read the Quran in iso-lation from the Sunnah. This reading wrongly con-siders the Sunnah to be a parallel or an alternative source of knowledge that could possibly be at odds with the Quranic commands. The Quran, however, confirms that the Sunnah is a *bayan* or illustration of the Quran. *"And We revealed to you [Muhammad] the Remembrance so that you may illustrate to the people what was sent down to them and that they might give thought."* (16:44)

2. Historical readings: In which a historical interpreta-tion of the original sources is taken from a textbook from the schools of law and considered to be the only possible interpretation. We will see examples of how some contemporary voices reject the renewal or re-interpretation of the original sources, the Quran and Sunnah, and insist on the superiority and rigid-ity of old opinions. However, the Quran and Sunnah

contain numerous commands that prohibit "blind following" of others without proof and independent judgement. Moreover, "renewal of the religion" is not a new term, but rather a term that was coined by the Prophet (s), when he stated: "Verily Allah sends to this ummah at the turn of every one hundred years people who will renew its religion."[8]

3. Historicist readings: In the name of rejecting stagnation and blind imitation of history, some people take the other extreme of "historicising" all interpretations and even the original sources themselves. Historicisation means the rejection of any everlasting "authority" or reference in the Word of Allah or the commands of His Messenger (s). They miss, however, that the Quran and the Prophetic example are not "cultural products" as is human speech or literature. The Quran and Sunnah are revealed knowledge suitable for every place and time.

A purpose-based and integrative reading of the Quran and the Sunnah is the methodology that we follow in this book. We move beyond partial readings to integrating all related views, contexts and sources into a purpose-based holistic reading. Purposes or the answers to the questions of 'why', represent the higher level of reasoning that resolves the contradicted and integrates the detached. We also move beyond the historical readings and interpretations by re-reading them in the current context and comparing them to contemporary opinions. Finally, we differentiate between the immutable articles of Islam, which cannot be "historicised" or altered, and the flexible articles, which can and should change with time and circumstances.

~

CHAPTER 3

*What does the Quran say about
women and mosques?*

There are dozens of Quranic verses related to mosques, all of
which urge all believers who seek guidance, light and knowledge, males and females alike, to frequent mosques. The following are a few examples:

> *"Say, O Muhammad, 'My Lord has ordered justice and
> that you all maintain yourselves in worship of Him at
> every mosque, and invoke Him, sincere to Him in re-
> ligion.'"* (7:29)

> *"O children of Adam, take your adornment at every
> mosque."* (7:31)

> *"The mosques of Allah are populated merely by those
> who believe in Allah and the Last Day and establish
> prayers and give charity and fear nothing except Allah,
> for it is expected that those are of the rightly guided."*
> (9:18)

> *"And the mosques are for Allah, so do not invoke with
> Allah anyone."* (72:18)

In addition, there are many verses in which Allah specif-
ically mentions the Sacred Mosque in Mecca, referring to it

as the "House of Allah" and the "Sacred House," and inviting all, men and women, to visit. Allah also mentioned by name the sacred mosque in Jerusalem, The Farthest Mosque. The following are a few examples:

> *"Behold! We gave to Abraham the site of the Sacred House, saying: 'Associate nothing in worship with Me; and sanctify My House for those who compass it round, or stand up, or bow, or prostrate themselves therein in prayer.' "* (22:26)

> *"Glory to Allah Who did take His servant for a journey by night from the Sacred Mosque to the Farthest Mosque."* (17:1)

> *"Allah made the Kaba, the Sacred House, an asylum of security for people [al-nas], as also the Sacred Months."* (5:97)

> *"Indeed, the first House of worship established for people [al-nas] was that at Mecca - blessed and a guidance for the worlds."* (3:96)

It is interesting to note that most of the English translators of these verses mentioned above, wrongly translate the Arabic words referring to the dwellers and visitors of the mosque to the English words "men" or "mankind." Take for example verse 3:96 mentioned above, which refers to the visitors of the mosque with the Arabic word "*al-nas*." This word means "the people" in every conventional and colloquial sense of the Arabic language. However, "al-nas" is rendered "men" or "mankind" by every major translator of the Quran, including: Muhammad Asad, Sahih International, Pickthall, Yusuf Ali,

Shakir, Muhammad Sarwar, and Mohsin Khan.[9] I am aware of one exception, Arberry, who translated "al-nas" in 3:96 as "the people." It is interesting that in verse 5:97 mentioned above, even Arberry translated "al-nas" to "men." This shows how the translators/interpreters of the Quran are influenced by their pre-assumptions and biases when it comes to the issue of women in the mosque.

However, there are two verses that urged believers to attend the mosque in which the word "*rijal*" was used to refer to mosque attendees:

> "*Such light is in mosques which Allah has ordered to be raised and that His name be mentioned therein; exalting Him within them in the morning and the evenings. [There are] persons [rijal] whom neither commerce nor sale distracts from the remembrance of Allah and performance of prayer and giving of charity.*" (24:36–37)

> "*A mosque founded on righteousness from the first day is more worthy for you to stand in. Within it are persons [rijal] who love to purify themselves; and Allah loves those who purify themselves.*" (9:108)

Some exegetes misunderstood the Arabic word "rijal" (which I translated above as "persons" in these two verses), and interpreted it to mean "men", to the exclusion of women. It is to be noted that every English translation of the Quran I am aware of translated this word as "men" except for Muhammad Sarwar who chose the word "people". The commonly used but wrong interpretation/translation had a negative impact on the collective perception of Muslims, who thought that there was no room for women in the mosque, according to the Quran.

The famous exegete Ibn Kathir (d. 774H/1373CE), for instance, commented on the word "rijal" in the verse quoted above from Surat Al-Nur, by saying:

> *"As for women, their praying at home is better for them ... But it is permissible for them to attend the congregational prayer offered by men, on condition that she does not harm any man by manifesting adornments or wearing perfume."[10]*

It is true that the word "rijal" in colloquial Arabic is used for males rather than females. However, in high Arabic, which is the language of the Quran, the word implies both males and females. This is evident in a number of verses in the Quran itself. For instance, Allah says, *"and on its elevations are rijal who recognise all by their mark"* (7:48), and *"Among the believers are rijal true to what they promised Allah."* (33:23)

In these two verses, and others, the word "rijal" is clearly referring to both males and females, and no scholar has ever disputed that.

In addition, linguistically speaking, when the Quranic address is specific to males only, the word "rijal" is coupled with the word *"nisa"* within the same sentence. In this case only, rijal means men and nisa means women. An example is verse 48:25: *"And if not for believing men (rijal) and believing women (nisa) whom you did not know..."* It is not possible to understand the Quran correctly without a good command of the Arabic language, and the best reference for the Arabic language is the Quran itself, which should override the colloquial usages of Arabic terms.

In addition to the Quranic evidence, Arabic-Arabic dictionaries unanimously agree that women could correctly be addressed by the word rijal. For instance, among the usages mentioned in *Mukhtar As-Sihah*,[11] a classic Arabic-Arabic dictionary under the entry "*R J L* (the root of the word rijal in Arabic)" is the following:

> *Niswatun rijal* (here, the word rijal is used as an adjective for females) ... and a woman can be called *rajulah* (singular female form of rijal) ... It is also reported that Aisha, may Allah be pleased with her, was known to be a rajulah in terms of her opinions.

In *Lisan Al-Arab*, another classic Arabic-Arabic dictionary, it is stated that: "In a reported conversation between Abu Zayd al-Killabi and his wife, the two "rijal" fiercely argued, referring to him and his wife."[12]

Finally, the Quran clearly forbids preventing people from frequenting the mosques, with Allah's saying,

> *"And who are more unjust than those who prevent people from mentioning the name of Allah in His mosques and strive toward their destruction. It is not for them to enter them except in fear. For them in this world is disgrace, and they will have in the Hereafter a great punishment."* (2:114).

However, today, half of the "people", i.e. women, are being prevented from mentioning the name of Allah in many of His mosques. The following chapters deal with other sides of the issue.

~

CHAPTER 4

What does the Sunnah say about
women and mosques?

The Sunnah of the Prophet (s) includes hundreds of authentic narrations indicating women's normal presence in the mosque at all times and on all occasions at the time of the Prophet (s). The following are a few examples:

I will start with a story that Imam Bukhari narrated after Aisha (r). It is the story of an African female slave who was freed by the Arab tribe that enslaved her, and eventually decided to "live" in a tent in the mosque of the Prophet (s). I am quoting the whole narration here because its details are worth reflecting upon. According to Aisha, the young African narrates:[13]

> "A baby girl from the tribe that had enslaved me came out wearing a red leather scarf decorated with precious stones. The scarf fell from her or she placed it somewhere. A bird passed by that place, saw the scarf on the ground and mistook it for a piece of meat. The bird took the scarf and flew away with it. The baby's family searched for the scarf and when they could not find it, they accused me of stealing it and started searching me aggressively. They even searched my private parts. By Allah, while I was being searched, the same bird returned

and dropped the red scarf on them. So I told them, 'This is what you accused me of and I was innocent. Here is your scarf.' "

Aisha added: "The family then freed that young lady, and she immediately came to Allah's Messenger (s) and embraced Islam. She then set up for herself a tent with a low roof in the mosque and lived in it. She used to visit me occasionally and chat with me. Every time she sat down with me, she would start by reciting the following poem:

The Day of the Scarf was one of my Lord's miracles.

With His Grace, He rescued me from the disbelievers."

Aisha added, "When I asked her once about the story of that poem, she told me the whole story."

In the above story, you can see how "normal" it was for the young lady to come and talk with the Prophet (s) in the mosque, and how she even lived in the mosque when she could not find shelter. By the way, Ibn Hazm, the Andalusian scholar, concluded based on this hadith that a woman's menses does not prevent her from staying in the mosque. More on that issue later.

Here are a few other narrations to reflect upon in the context of women in the mosque of the Prophet (s):

Aisha (r) said: "Sa'd Ibn Muaz was wounded on the Battle of the Al-Khandaq (The Ditch) … Then, the Prophet (s) set up a tent in the mosque for Sa'd to be able to visit frequently."[14]

Commenting on this particular narration, Ibn Hajar, stated that: "The Messenger of Allah (s) actually let Sa'd stay in Rufaydah's tent in the mosque. She was known for her skills in treating the wounded. The Prophet (s) said, 'let Sa'd stay in her tent so that I can visit him from a close distance.' "[15]

Rufaydah was a female companion and a physician who

set up a tent in the Prophet's mosque. This tent is known to be the first emergency clinic in Islam's history.

Imam Muslim mentions that Al-Sha'bi narrated: "We entered upon Fatimah bint Qays, and she said, 'It was announced that the people should gather for prayer, and then I was among those heading for the Prophet's Mosque. I was in the front row of women, which was right behind the last row of men, when I heard the Prophet (s) saying while he was on the pulpit: 'The cousins of Al-Dary sailed the sea ...' "[16]

Bukhari narrated that Asma bint Abu Bakr said: "I came to Aisha, may Allah be pleased with her, the wife of the Prophet (s) when the sun had eclipsed, and found out that all people were standing in prayer...when the Prophet (s) finished the prayer, he thanked and praised Almighty Allah."[17]

Asma bint Abu Bakr narrates the same story as follows: "The sun eclipsed during the lifetime of the Prophet (s), peace be upon him...then, I came and entered the mosque, and saw the Messenger of Allah (s) standing up in prayer. I joined him in prayer, but he kept standing up so long that I felt I needed to sit down. Yet, I would notice a weak woman standing next to me, and then I would say to myself, "She is even weaker than me" and I would keep standing...Then he (s) bowed down in *ruku* and kept bowing for a long time, and then he raised his head from ruku and kept standing up for a very long time. A man approached then and, because of the delay, thought that the Prophet (s) had not yet offered the ruku."[18]

Bukhari and others narrated that Aisha (r) said: "The believing women, covered with their veiling sheets, used to attend the dawn prayer with Allah's Messenger, and after finishing the prayer they would return to their homes."[19]

Umm Salamah, the wife of the Prophet (s), narrates that

during the lifetime of the Prophet (s), when women had concluded the ordained prayer, they would rise and leave, and the Prophet (s) would sometimes stay along with the men.[20]

Moreover, it was narrated from Asma: "I heard the Prophet (s) saying, 'Whoever of you women believes in Allah and in the Last Day should not raise her head until we men raise our heads after prostration, lest they should see the private parts of men.' " Asma added: "This was because their lower garments were short, knowing that most of them at the time could only afford to wear a *namirah* (a small lower garment)."[21]

Asma also narrated: "The Messenger of Allah (s) stood up amongst us and preached to us, mentioning the questions that a dead person would be asked in the grave, and thereupon the people clamoured in a manner that prevented me from perceiving the concluding words of the Messenger of Allah. When they calmed down, I asked a man sitting in front of me, 'May Allah bless you, what did the Messenger say concluding his sermon?' He answered, 'It was revealed to me that you would be tested in your graves in a manner almost similar to that of *Al-Dajjal* trial.' "[22]

Abu Hurairah narrated that a black woman who used to clean the mosque, died. When the Messenger (s) asked about her, they informed him that she had died. He then said, "Why did you not inform me when she died? Guide me to her grave." So, he approached her grave and offered the funeral prayer for her there.[23]

Moreover, it was narrated from Aisha (r) that when Sa'd Ibn Abu Waqqas died, the wives of the Prophet (s) sent a message to bring his bier into the mosque so that they should offer prayer for him.[24]

Atikah bint Zayd, Umar Ibn Al-Khattab's wife, used to offer the *fajr* (dawn) and the *isha* (night) prayers in congregation in the mosque. Some attendees of the mosque asked her, "Why do you come out for the prayer even though you know that Umar dislikes it? It makes him jealous." She replied, "Then, why does not he forbid me from doing that?" They answered, "What prevents him is the statement of Allah's Messenger (s) 'Do not prevent women from going to Allah's mosques.'"[25] Ibn Hajar commented: "Indeed, when Umar was stabbed, Atikah was in the mosque praying behind him."[26]

Finally, Bukhari and Muslim narrated after Aisha (r), the Prophet's wife:

> "Allah's Apostle invited me on a day of Eid to watch the Abyssinians who were playing in the mosque, displaying their skill with spears. He asked: Would you like to watch? I answered: 'Yes.' So I stood behind him and he lowered his shoulder so I can put my chin on it. I did and leaned with my face on his cheek and watched. Eventually, he asked me several times if I wanted to leave and I replied every time: 'Please wait.' I was not interested in watching, really, but on that day I wanted women especially to know my status with him. Therefore, appreciate a young lady's keenness to be playful."[27]

I must add here the following note: in this hadith, which took place shortly after Aisha's marriage to the Prophet (s), she was not a "young girl" as some commentators claimed. My estimate of Aisha's age when she married the Prophet (s) in the first year of the Hijri Calendar, is 19, not nine as some scholars claimed. This is based on a long investigation of different historical narrations related to her age, the details of which are beyond the scope of this book. However, I decided to give a brief outline of my argument below. This discussion is relevant to this book about women in the mosque, especially from a methodological point of view.

A non-authentic narration, which was unfortunately included in the authentic collections (Bukhari No. 3894 and Muslim No. 1422), indicated that the Prophet (s) consummated his marriage to Aisha when she was "nine years old". There is no difference of opinion over the fact that this marriage took place in Medina in the first year after Hijra. However, there are other authentic narrations, also in the same Bukhari and Muslim authentic collections, which logically contradict the "nine years old" narration.

For example, Bukhari's narration (No. 2724) that Aisha participated with the Muslim army in the Battle of Uhud (in Year 2 Hijri) means that she was supposedly 10 years old during that battle. This is logically impossible, given her role in battle that was narrated in the hadith. This narration also contradicts with numerous other narrations in which the Prophet (s) never allowed children under 15 to witness battles.

Bukhari himself also narrates (No. 2176) that Aisha witnessed her father's attempt to migrate to Abyssinia, which was during Year 4 of the Message (Year 9 Before Hijra) according to all accounts. This witnessing could not have happened before Aisha herself was born, as the "nine years old" hadith implies!

Bukhari himself also narrates (No. 4595) that Aisha witnessed the revelation of Surat Al-Qamar (Chapter 54) while she was a "*jariyah*" (an Arabic term for a girl between 6 and 13) "playing in Mecca". Chapter 54 was revealed somewhere between the Years 2 and 4 of the Message (i.e. between Years 11 and 9 Before Hijra), according to all other accounts. This means that in the first year after Hijra, her age must have been somewhere between 15 and 24, according to the simple mathematical logic of these Bukhari narrations themselves.

Other narrations, by Ibn Ishaq this time, show that Aisha was the "19th person to embrace Islam" in the first year of the message (i.e. 13 years Before Hijra), and that she was a "young girl" at that time (Ibn Hisham, 271). Ibn Ishaaq was rendered "trustworthy" by many, including Imams Sufian Al-Thawri, Al-Zuhri, Shu'ba, Al-Shafie, Ali Ibn Al-Madini, and other prominent scholars. It is true that Imam Malik and Hisham Ibn Urwa accused Ibn Ishaq of lying, but many other scholars disagreed, especially as Malik never met Ibn Ishaq himself.

In fact, it is Hisham Ibn Urwa, whom I think is the source of the error in the "nine years old" narrations. He was accused of lying (*tadlees*) by a number of scholars, including Malik Ibn Anas and Ibn Hajar, and of having developed amnesia later in his life by other scholars, including Yahya Ibn Saeed and Ibn Khirash. His conduct with the Umayyad kings of his time also shows lack of integrity and honesty.[28]

To me, Hisham Ibn Urwa's serious problem is his narration about the Prophet (s) being a victim of some magic spell (*hadith sihr al-rasul*). Hisham is the source of the claim that the Prophet (s) fell under some magic spell that was made by an unknown Jewish young man from Medina by the name Labid Ibn A'sam (Bukhari No. 4530). Hisham claimed that to the Prophet (s) spent some time, "imagining that he did things that he never did," etc. This narration by Hisham contradicts many Quranic principles, including Allah's promise to *"protect the Prophet from people"* (5:67), and the Quran's repeated rejection of claims from the pagans of Mecca that the Prophet (s) was under a magical spell (refer to: 17:47, 17:101, and 25:8). For me, this narration alone makes Hisham non-trustworthy, despite the greatness of his father Urwah Ibn Al-Zubair, who was one of the seven most prominent jurists of Medina, and his grandfather Al-Zubair Ibn Al-Awwam, a prominent companion of the Prophet (s).

We also have the other authentic narrations that Aisha was briefly "engaged" to Jubair Ibn Mut'am Ibn 'Adiyy (Ahmad's Collection, No. 25810), before she married the Prophet (s) – an engagement that could not have happened logically before the age of 6 or 7, as Hisham's narration implies! And there is another historical fact that Aisha was ten years younger than her sister Asma Bint Abu Bakr, and Asma was 17 (or otherwise 27 according to other narrations) in the first year of the message when she embraced Islam. This puts Aisha's age around seven in the first year of the Message (13 Before Hijra). Therefore Aisha was at least 19 when she married the Prophet (s), peace be upon him.

Finally, when we have such contradictions in narrations transferred by "trustworthy" narrators, we must apply the method of critiquing the content (*naqd al-matn*). This means that the Prophet's marrying Aisha at the age of 19 is more likely to have happened than marrying a girl literally in her childhood (at the age of six, seven or nine, narrations differ). This critique has a specific significance because the narrations related to this marriage have been cited in fatwa (legal ruling) about marriage age in Islam. The fatwa that allowed the marriage of children at the age of nine has caused the demise of numerous poor girls in our time and before. I must add that my view is not based on a bias to any particular western or eastern "culture," legal or social, but is purely based on the understanding (*dirayah*) of the narrations and the rules of *fiqh* (jurisprudence) of marriage in Islam and its higher objectives (*maqasid*). If marriage is about achieving the objectives of "mutual love and mercy," as the Quran asserts (30:21), how can marrying a six or nine year old girl achieve mutual love and mercy?

The same higher objectives of the Sharia and holistic understanding of the Sunnah narrations are essential for us to be able to answer the remaining questions in this book, prime of which is the next question: if this is the status of women in the Prophet's Mosque, on what basis do some Muslims prevent women from the mosque?

CHAPTER 5

*On what basis do some Muslims prevent
women from entering the mosques?*

Al-Tabarani narrates:

"Bilal Ibn Abdullah Ibn Omar Ibn Al-Khattab narrated to me that one day his father Abdullah Ibn Omar
said: 'Indeed, I heard the Messenger of Allah (s) say,
"Do not deprive the female slaves of Allah of their
share in the mosques.'" Bilal said, "As for me, I shall
forbid my household females, but whosoever wishes
to let his women go out, let him do so." Thus, my father Abdullah turned to Bilal and said, "May Allah
curse you! May Allah curse you! May Allah curse
you! You hear me say that the Messenger of Allah ordered that women are not to be deprived, and you
say otherwise." Abdullah wept and angrily departed."

Another narration stated that Abdullah, "stretched his
hand and slapped Bilal."29

A similar report was narrated by Al-Tirmidhi:

"We were at Ibn Omar's, when he said, the Messenger
of Allah said, 'Permit women to go to mosques at night.'
His son said, 'By Allah, we would not permit them to do
so as they would do mischief.' Ibn Omar replied, 'I say

that the Messenger said such and such, and you say, 'we would not allow them?' "[30]

Here, the reaction of Abdullah Ibn Omar (r), who narrated the quoted hadith, indicates clearly the prohibition of preventing women from visiting the mosque, a prevention that is contrary to the Prophet's command. But Bilal, his son, wanted to avoid what he called "mischief" (*daghal, fitnah*), and applied the method that was later known as "blocking the means" or "cutting the roots" (*sadd al-dhara'i'*). This is consequentialist logic in prohibiting something lawful in order to prevent something unlawful from happening.

I made an extensive survey on various schools of Islamic jurisprudence, and concluded that scholars who prevented or discouraged women from going to the mosques generally ignored the clarity of Abdullah Ibn Omar's narration and reaction, and relied instead on one or both of the following two narrations in support of their view:

1. Aisha (r) said, "If the Messenger of Allah (s) had seen the unlawful innovations that women have introduced, he would have definitely prevented them from going to the mosque, as the women of the Children of Israel were prevented from their temples."[31]

2. Umm Humaid, a companion, narrated that the Prophet (s) told her: "Your prayer in your house is better for you than your prayer in the congregation."[32] So, her nephew narrates, Umm Humaid ordered that a prayer place be prepared for her in the furthest and darkest part of her house, and she used to pray there until she died."[33]

As for Aisha's (r) opinion, it is obvious that her statement was made in a particular context, the context of some women who were committing some unlawful acts in the mosque. She did not mean to change the default recommendation or "abrogate" it, in the sense that was understood by some jurists. No jurist in Medina during her time judged that her statement indicated a change in the default ruling of permissibility. Soon after her time, when Imam Malik of Medina was asked his opinion about preventing women from visiting the mosque, he said, "Women should never be prevented from going out to the mosques."[34]

Ibn Hajar commented:

"Some scholars held on to Aisha's prevention of women's frequenting the mosque as absolute, though it is debatable. For it does not entail a change in the ruling since she made it contingent on a non-existent condition, "if he had seen … he would have prevented," but he (s) neither saw nor prevented. Besides, these innovations were introduced only by a few, not all, women. Hence, if prevention is necessary, it would apply only to them."[35]

Ibn Hazm has a similar argument:

"Certainly, some women only, and not all, introduced these unlawful innovations. It is impossible to prevent goodness for those who did not do such things because of those who committed them."[36]

Ibn Qudamah also said:

"The Prophet's Sunnah is more worthy to be followed, and Aisha's, may Allah be pleased with her, statement is limited only to those who introduce unlawful innovations."[37]

It is clear from these examples, and many others, that taking what Aisha (r) said as a general rule is an extreme interpretation that no sound scholar would approve.

On the other hand, in today's context, restrictions and obstacles hindering women from visiting the mosque should be removed, not the other way around. Women should in fact be encouraged to go to the mosque, not only as her right, but also as this serves many good purposes, including remembering Allah, acquiring knowledge, meeting other Muslim women who frequent the mosque, and participating in public activities in a way that benefits her, her religion, her family, her community.

In terms of Islamic jurisprudence, means have to be "opened" instead of being "blocked". Theorists of *fiqh* have proposed "opening the means" (*fat-h al-dhara'i'*) as an alternative methodology to "blocking" them when circumstances differ.[38] The Maliki scholar Al-Qarafi, for example, explained that the means which lead to prohibited ends should be blocked and discouraged, whereas means that lead to lawful ends should be opened and encouraged.[39] Ibn Farhun, for another example, applied 'opening the means' to a number of rulings.[40]

Finally, Sheikh Abdul-Halim Abu Shuqqah commented on Aisha's (r) opinion by a call to opening the means, rather than blocking them, for women in the mosque. He writes:

"Had Aisha, may Allah be pleased with her, seen the unlawful innovations that the women of our time have introduced in places of entertainment and sports, had she witnessed the vicious media invasion that manip-ulates their minds and hearts, and had she witnessed that fact today that the only place where women are not allowed is the mosque – would she have made the same judgment? The answer is no. In fact, Aisha would have said, 'Had the Messenger, peace be upon him, seen what is happening, he would have made it obligatory for women to frequent the mosque.' She would have encouraged women to frequent mosques with the same zeal she had to deter them from the mosque before. She would have been keen for women to avoid temptations and learn good habits by asking them to visit the mosques."[41]

We will deal, next, with the second narration about Umm Humaid that was mentioned above, and attempt to answer the question: Did the Prophet (s) say that a woman's prayer at home is better than at the mosque?

~

CHAPTER 6

Did the Prophet (s) say that a woman's prayer
at home is better than at the mosque?

No, not for all women, nor in all times. The hadith quoted in
the previous chapter, which was narrated by Ibn Hibban and
Ahmad about Umm Humaid ("your prayer at home is better
than your prayer in congregation") is authentic, but incom-
plete. The context or the full story of the hadith was not explained in the famous narrations.

However, the other narrators of the same story, name-
ly, Al-Tabarani, Al-Baihaqi, Ibn Abu Shaibah, and Ibn Abu
Asim, gave more detail. Their (authentic) additions explained
that the context of the hadith was an argument between Umm
Humaid and Abu Humaid Al-Saedi, her husband. The argument was due to Um Humaid's regular attendance of congregational prayer in the Prophet's Mosque. In these narrations,
Umm Humaid visited the Prophet (s) with a group of women
and said, "O Messenger of Allah, we like to pray with you but
our husbands prevent us from coming to the mosque."[42]

Abu Humaid Al-Saedi was from the family of Bani Saedah,
a branch of Al-Khazraj tribe in Medina. They used to live far
from the Prophet's Mosque, beyond the borders of Medina
at the time, and had their own farms, their own Bani Saedah
Council (*saqeefat bani saedah*) and their own mosque, which
the Prophet (s) visited once and prayed in. (Ibn Majah No. 1217)

Therefore, the Messenger of Allah (s) only intended to re-
solve a marital disagreement between Umm Humaid and Abu
Humaid, which was over the long distance she had to walk
five times a day to pray behind him in his mosque. The Prophet (s) basically advised Umm Humaid to accommodate her
husband's request, for the sake of her children and family, and
pray in the tribe's mosque or at home.

There is no evidence that the Prophet (s) meant to change
the default rule for women to visit mosques, or even the special reward for praying in his mosque (s), which he mentioned
in several other narrations for visitors to his mosque – men
and women. This is the only possible interpretation that resolves the conflict between the different hadiths. The basic
juridical rule states that the application of all scripts is better
than neglecting any of them.

I do have an issue, however, with the narrations stating
that Umm Humaid chose the "darkest" and "furthest" spot in
her house to pray in. I believe that, if these narrations were
true, it was Umm Humaid's preference to choose that spot
rather than the Prophet's instruction (s). There are hundreds
of other narrations that include women praying in congregation, and none of them included a recommendation to choose
a "dark" or a "far" spot.

Other than the hadith of Umm Humaid discussed above,
there is no other authentic narration that could have implied
discouraging or preventing women from visiting the mosque,
or a general rule that their praying at home is better than
praying in the Prophet's Mosque itself. In fact, the Prophet (s)
famously said: "One prayer in this mosque of mine is better
than one thousand prayers elsewhere, except for the Sacred
Mosque in Mecca."[43] The Prophet (s) in this recommendation

made no differentiation between men and women.

However, some scholars, advocating the prevention of women from frequenting the mosque, have relied on a number of non-authentic narrations as supporting evidence! Yet, such weak narrations do not constitute solid proof or countermand the numerous authentic hadiths supporting the contrary opinion.

Let us discuss one example of these non-authentic narrations, which unfortunately appear in numerous contemporary fatwas related to women and visiting the mosque.[44] It is the narration that claims that the Prophet (s) asked his daughter Fatimah what is best for a woman. The narration claims that Fatimah answered, "that she should see no man and that no man should see her." The Prophet (s), according to the narration, then hugged her and said, "good offspring descending from one another."[45] In addition to its weak chain of narration (*isnad*), the meaning of this hadith contradicts with many explicit statements of the Quran about women's interaction with men in various circumstances and events, including the verse in which Allah included the children of the Prophet (s), including Fatimah, in one of those events:

> *"Then whoever argues with you Muhammad about it after this knowledge has come to you – say, 'Come, let us call our children and your children, our wives and your wives, ourselves and yourselves, then supplicate earnestly together and invoke the curse of Allah upon the liars among us.' "* (3:61)

This verse explicitly mentions the children of the Prophet (s). Ibn Kathir commented on the verse, and mentioned the story of the delegation to Najran, stating:

"They refused to acknowledge the truth. Then, when dawn broke, the Prophet (s) after informing them of the newly revealed verses, came out with Al-Hasan and Al-Husain wrapped in a velvet cloth of his, and Fatimah came out walking behind him."[46]

There are also numerous other hadiths that involve Fatimah (r) "seen" in public in various contexts and dealing with men in a normal way.

Finally, it is to be noted that a woman's visit to the mosque, and a man's visit as well, is not supposed to compromise other duties that are of higher priority. This consideration is relative, of course, subject to individuals and families and their specific circumstances. That is why the Prophet (s), as discussed earlier, recommended that Umm Humaid stay closer to her family, and as discussed later, he did not require from women to pray the Friday prayer in the mosque as he required from men. There is a special consideration given to women, given their various family and care-giving circumstances, especially mothers with small children. The general rule, however, is that it is impermissible to prevent women from going out to the mosque, if they wish to, and that her performing of a regular prayer in the mosque is better and more rewarding than her praying at home or anywhere else.

~

CHAPTER 7

Are the hadith narrations that ridicule women true?
Are most women "dwellers of hell"?

There are a few, and unfortunately popular, narrations that appear to ridicule women. These problematic narrations have impacted on the perception of the role of women in Islam in general and in the mosque in particular. However, such narrations go against the principles that the Quran sets for women's dignity and rights, and against the overwhelming evidence of numerous other narrations about the Prophet's dealing with women and the high status he (s) gave them. As we will see below, such narrations are either erroneously claimed to be uttered by the Prophet (s), or they are true sayings that were (mis)interpreted in isolation of their context and true meaning.

One example of such narrations, which is the basis of some objections to a common space for men and women in the mosque, is a claim that a man's prayer is nullified if a woman passes in front of him, including in the mosque. Some scholars even believe that a man who sees a woman passing in front of him has to quit his prayer and repeat it.[47]

Imams Muslim and Ahmad narrated that Abu Hurairah (r) reported that the Prophet (s) said, "Prayer is interrupted by a woman, a dog or a donkey, when they pass in front of a praying person."[48] In addition to the fact that this narration contradicts with numerous other authentic reports about the

Prophet's Mosque, it is in conflict with other reports that indicate the exact opposite, some of which were reported by the same companion, Abu Hurairah.

It was reported that Abu Hurairah narrated that the Prophet (s) said, "A person's prayer is *not* interrupted by a woman, a dog, or a donkey, and push back whoever passes closely in front of you while you are praying."[49] This contradiction between two "authentic" narrations simply means that there is an error in one of them.

We have another report by Aisha (r), the Mother of the Believers, where she criticises the first narration as inaccurate:

> "Abdullah Ibn Ubaidillah Ibn Omair reported that when Aisha was asked about the narration that the passing of a dog, a woman, or a donkey interrupts a man's prayer, she stated, 'Why are you mentioning Muslim women in the same context with these animals?' In another narration, she said, 'How come you hold us equal to a donkey and a dog?' and in a third narration, 'I have witnessed occasions in which I would wake up while the Prophet (s) was offering prayer with me lying interposed between him and the qiblah like the bier of a corpse in a funeral prayer.' "[50]

Al-Shafi rejected Abu Huraira's first narration as erroneous, and commented on Aisha's objection to the narration by saying, "If a woman's presence in front of a praying person does not invalidate his prayer, then her passing in front of him does not invalidate it either."[51] Muhammad Ibn Al-Hassan Al-Shaibani commented on the same narration, "This means that there is no harm if a man prays while his wife is lying, standing or sitting in front of him or to his side."[52]

Abu Dawud noted the conflicting reports on this issue despite the practice of the companions, may Allah be pleased with them, and said, "If two reports from the Prophet (s) conflict, we should refer to the established practice of his companions after him."[53] The established practice of his companions never implied any objection to men or women walking in the mosque while others, men or women, pray.

Another example of such popular but erroneous narrations is, according to Bukhari, when Abu Hurairah (r) narrated, "Your bad omen is in your house and your woman."[54] A number of commentators interpreted this hadith to imply that a man is under the effect of a bad omen if his house is far from the mosque or his woman is barren.[55]

It is interesting to note that many jurists, past and present, approved this hadith simply because it is in the Bukhari collection, even though Bukhari himself also narrated, in a different hadith in the same book, "there is no such thing as a bad omen."[56]

And commenting on Abu Hurairah's narration, Aisha (r) said: "Abu Hurairah did not recall this correctly. The Prophet (s) was praying against those who claimed that bad omens are in a house, a woman, and a horse. Abu Huraira came late and heard only the last part of the hadith and did not hear the first part."[57]

In terms of the science of hadith, Aisha (r) rejected Abu Hurairah's narration on the basis of the weakness of its content (*matn*) rather than the weakness of its chain of narrators (*sanad*). Abu Hurairah is a great companion, but he simply made a mistake in this narration. Apparently, he did not hear the complete statement, and he thought he did.[58] But Ibn al-Jawzi, surprisingly, commented: "How can Aisha reject an authentic narration?" and Ibn Al-Arabi, shockingly, commented: "Aisha's rejection of the narration is nonsense."[59] To me, Ibn al-Jawzi and Ibn Al-Arabi were too blinded by imitation to accept the Mother of the Believers' assessment of this strange narration. Badruddin Al-Zarkashi and Jalaluddin Al-Suyuti, on the other hand, were inspired by her opinion. Each of them wrote a whole book dedicated to Aisha's critiques and corrections of other companions' narrations, in which they cited dozens of such amendments including the "bad omens" narration.[60]

Our third example is a misinterpreted narration, which is often quoted to also discourage women from visiting the mosque. This is the following narration by Abu Hurairah:

> "I heard the Prophet (s) say, 'The best of men's rows are the front rows and their worst are their rear rows, while women's best rows are their back rows and their worst are their front rows.' "[61]

Some people draw on this hadith to prevent women from praying in the mosque at all, to isolate them in separate halls, or push them to the back of the mosque. They interpret the hadith to imply that women who pray in the mosque somehow commit an evil deed, because their front rows are the "worst rows."

This is a strange interpretation. The hadith rather asserts the preference of men's standing in the first rows and women's standing in the last rows in prayer, nothing else. This preference was made for the following three considerations:

1. The front men's row and the rear women's row are the ones filled by those who come earlier to mosque,

which is a well-known virtue. Refer to the next two chapters that will explain the way the Prophet's mosque was designed and rows were filled.

2. These two rows close to the walls of the mosque help the praying person, man or woman, to avoid distractions that may take place in the middle of the mosque, and this entails the virtue of uninterrupted concentration in prayers.

3. This instruction is in harmony with other hadiths in which the Prophet (s) forbade praying women from raising their heads from prostration before men. This was in order to give men enough time to cover themselves properly as they stood. Due to the poor economic situation at the time, not all companions could afford clothes that were long enough to cover them during prostration. Asma narrated: "I heard the Prophet (s) say, 'Whoever of you believes in Allah and in the Last Day should not raise her head until the men raise their heads after prostration,' lest they should see the private parts of men because their lower garments were short."[62]

Amr Ibn Salamah narrated a related story:

"Some companions were looking for a person to lead the prayers, and found no one who knew more Quran than I did. I used to memorise the Quran during my travels with the caravans. They therefore made me their imam. At that time I was a boy of six or seven years, wearing a *burdah* [a black square garment]. It was so short that when I prostrated, it exposed my body. A lady from the tribe said, "Won't you cover the privates of your reciter for us?" So they bought a piece of cloth and made a coat for me. I had never been so happy with anything as I was with that coat."[63]

The above story explains the hadith and corrects the misinterpretation. The matter of "best" and "worst" rows is not about men versus women, but rather about a number of practical considerations in organising the congregational prayers in the mosque.

Our fourth and final example is another narration that will require some detailed discussion in order to clear a popular, negative and unfair misconception about women. Jabir Ibn Abdullah (r) reported, according to Bukhari:

"I attended Eid Prayer with the Messenger of Allah. He started with the prayer before the sermon, without an *Adhan* or an *Iqamah*. Then, he stood up, and while leaning on Bilal, commanded people to fear Allah and obey His commands. He started with the men and advised them, and then walked towards the women and advised them. He said: 'Give charity'... Women started giving out their jewellery in charity, throwing their earrings and rings in Bilal's garment."[64]

I find it an unavoidable duty on myself to add a note here to critique this particular hadith, even though some readers might find my note offensive, given the high status of the Bukhari collection. I have to confirm that Imam Bukhari did a superb job in compiling his collection, but he and his narrators are not infallible. This is especially evident when Imam Bukhari's own narrations contradict each other or contradict the Quran in a way that is beyond conciliation, which happened a few times in his outstanding book.

In every collection of hadith, events are typically narrated in a number of different ways, with a difference of two or three words between different accounts. Sometimes they have no bearing on the meaning of the hadith, whereas at others the difference is as contrary as one sentence being compatible with the Quranic principles and the moral model of the Prophet (s), and another sentence – with one word less or more – implying quite the opposite.

In this particular hadith, and after the Prophet's instruction for women to "give charity" as narrated above, he talked with women about hellfire. That was the sequence of his speech according to dozens of narrations and accounts of that day.[65]

However, narrations differed in some significant details. The most famous is Bukhari's wordings quoted above according to Jabir, in which it is claimed that after he said "give charity," the Prophet (s) directed his speech to his female companions to say: "Give charity, for I saw that you were the majority of the dwellers of hell" (*tasaddaqn fi'inni ra'aytukunn akthar ahl al-nar*).

In other narrations, it is claimed that the Prophet (s) talked about hellfire and the majority of women in general, not this particular group of female companions. In the Bukhari collection too (No. 29), another narration says: "I was shown hell, and I found that most of its dwellers are women" (*ureet al-nar fa idha akthar ahliha al-nisa*).

There are a couple of dozen similar narrations, in Bukhari and in other sources, with wordings that imply one of the above two meanings. In these narrations, it is claimed that the women then asked why this was the case, and the answer was: "Women are ungrateful to their spouses" (*yakfurn al-'asheer*), or, addressing the female companions: "You curse too much and you are ungrateful to your spouses" (*tukthirn al-la'n wa takfurn al-'asheer*).

I find the above two groups of narrations to be highly problematic and not making sense in the context of a speech on a day of Eid! More significantly, they do not fit the sensitivity and high manners of the Prophet (s) that the Quran confirmed and that he (s) demonstrated in numerous other instances when dealing with women. How is it possible that the Prophet (s) during a celebration of Eid tells his female companions, whom the Quran praised highly in clear terms,[66] that most of them are dwellers of hell? What sense does this make?

It is unfortunate that this false conception and assumed "fact" that most dwellers of hell are women, as implied by these narrations, has had quite a negative impact on Muslim cultures and the general understanding of the status of women in Islam.

However, there are a couple of other narrations, in the Bukhari collection and in others, which conveyed a slightly different wording of the Prophet's speech, albeit with quite a different meaning. Earlier in the very same Bukhari collection (No. 29), another narration that is according to Abdullah Ibn Abbas this time states: "I was shown hell, and most of the dwellers I saw were disbelieving women" (*ureet al-nar fa idha akthar ahliha al-nisa yakfurn.*). The rest of the narration, which describes those "disbelieving women" as individuals who curse everything and are ungrateful to their spouses, now makes sense. Here the Prophet (s) is telling his female companions about some disbelieving women who are dwellers of hell, not that *they* or women *in general* are dwellers of hell.

In fact, in other narrations, in Ibn Hibban's authentic collection for example, the Prophet (s) added an example of one of those women who were "dwellers of hell." He described, "a tall woman from Himyar, who tied and starved her cat with no food or drink, and would not let her eat anything including the insects on the ground" (*imra'ah min himyar tuwalah rabatat hirrah laha lam tut'imha wa lam tasqiha wa lam tada'ha ta'kul min khashash al-ardh*).[67] The woman who starved her cat to death is indeed one of the "dwellers of hell", not the Prophet's female companions, and not women in general!

It is unfortunate that these narrations mentioned above, and a few others, had quite a negative impact on the popular perception of the status of women in Islam, and caused many people, Muslims and non-Muslims, young and old, to reject the faith altogether. We have seen, however, that women do not "annul" men's prayers when they pass through the mosque, women are not "bad omens," women do not form the "worst rows" in the mosque, nor are women the "majority of dwellers of hell". All of these are misquoted and misunderstood narrations. The status of women in Islam, and in the mosque, is a status of dignity and equality. There are numerous evidences for this fact from the Prophet's example (s). Additional evidence is presented in the following chapters.

~

CHAPTER 8

How did the Prophet (s) design the
first mosque in Medina?

The design of the Prophet's Mosque in Medina is absent everywhere in the world today, including Medina itself. In the Arab countries, it is common to see men's prayer rooms totally separate from women's, especially in parks and public spaces. Sometimes there is quite a walking distance between the two prayer rooms in the same venue. In larger mosques, women pray in separate halls, smaller side rooms or balconies attached to the building of the mosque. The separation between men and women's prayer areas is strict, and women have little access, if any, to the main halls.

Mosques in the West that designate areas for women rarely allow women to line up directly behind men in the same hall, as was the practice in the Prophet's Mosque during his lifetime and for centuries thereafter. Western mosques usually contain special halls or side areas for women, in the basement, in a small room, in a balcony inside or outside the mosque, or in a secondary building attached to the mosque. Loudspeakers are usually used to communicate the imam's voice to the women's areas, and there is a growing trend of using internal cameras to show the imam on a screen installed in the women's area. Women's side entrances are clearly separated from the "men's entrances," which are the main entrances to the mosques.

In the Indian sub-continent, women do not have spaces inside regular mosques at all, nor do they have separate mosques. They all have to pray at home. In China, however, women-only mosques are popular amongst Chinese Muslims and they regularly have women imams. In Africa, all of the above models exist, but women pray in isolated areas in most cases.

There are seven problems in confining women to "women's areas" in isolation from the "men's areas":

1. Women's areas are always much smaller than the main prayer hall, which is always dedicated to men. Women's areas are usually overcrowded especially during Friday prayer and other occasions, while men's prayer areas and halls are often far from full. This is despite the growing phenomenon today that women outnumber men in Islamic activities and celebrations, especially in countries where Muslims are a minority.

2. Women's halls are usually not as nicely furnished or equipped as men's halls, in terms of carpets, lights, sound devices and facilities. Hence, women feel less welcome and less privileged than men in all mosques, with very few exceptions.

3. Children usually accompany their mothers or female caregivers within women's spaces. This causes much distraction to women who come to pray in congregation and makes women's areas much noisier than men's.

4. Women are never allowed to enter mosques through the main "men's entrance". Their entrances are always narrow entrances at the side or the back of the mosque.

5. Women cannot see the imam directly, and therefore cannot maintain contact or direct communication, and cannot follow him if he makes an extra prostration while reciting the Quran (*sajdat tilawah*). Most women attendees never know who the imam is because they never see him.

6. If women lose the sound connection to their area, they lose the continuity of following the imam in the sermon or prayer, and they have to break their prayer.

7. Last but not least, all of the above gives a clear impression to everyone, especially non-Muslim visitors and the new generation of Muslim youth, that "Islam" marginalises and/or isolates women. The result is that women are less involved in the affairs of the community, even if they were to attend the mosque.

At the beginning of this book, we asked: what is "Islamic"? And how do we learn about it? And the answer is to follow the example of the Prophet (s) since he was the best interpreter of the Quran and the leader of the Muslim community.

The *maquette* below illustrates the general design of the Prophet's mosque during his lifetime. The Prophet (s) built the mosque in Rabi-ul-Awwal of the first Hijri year (622 CE). It was nearly 35 metres long and 30 metres wide with a ceiling approximately 2.5 metres high. The walls were built from simple clay bricks. A few trunk pillars held the (partial) ceiling together, which was made out of palm-tree crowns and leafs.

In the Prophet's Mosque, there were three entrances, one of which led to a corridor connected to the Prophet's rooms (*hujuraat*) on the eastern side, and the other two led to the open area outside the mosque. There were no barriers, curtains or partitions, despite their availability. The Prophet's rooms themselves had partitioning curtains for the privacy of the Mothers of the Believers, but no partitioning curtain was ever placed inside the Prophet's Mosque.[68]

In terms of the organisation of rows, they are illustrat-

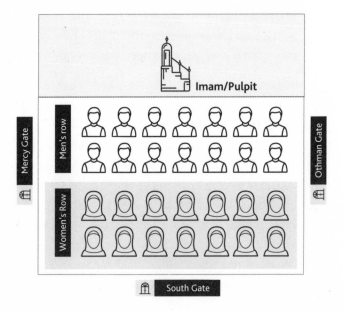

ed by the drawing below. The established Sunnah throughout the Prophet's life was that men formed rows right behind the Prophet (s) starting from the first row behind him. Women's rows started at the rear of the mosque and were added forward, as illustrated.

Children who attended the prayers would line up in rows between the men's and women's rows. Men's and women's rows were not separated by buildings, walls or curtains, though this could have been done. Rather, the last of men's rows was directly in front of the women's front row, as mentioned in many hadiths.

Urwah Ibn Al-Zubair narrated from Asma that she said:

"The Messenger of Allah (s) stood up amongst us and preached to us, mentioning the questioning a dead person faces in the grave. Thereupon people clamoured in a manner that prevented me from hearing the concluding words of the Messenger of Allah. When they calmed down, I asked a man sitting in front of me, 'May Allah bless you, what did the Messenger (s) say concluding his sermon?' He answered, 'It was revealed to me that you would be tested in your graves in a manner almost similar to that of Al-Dajjal's trial.' "[69]

Fatimah bint Qays narrated,

"It was announced publically that people should gather for prayer, and then I was among those heading to the mosque...I was in the front row of women, which was right behind the last row of men, when I heard the Prophet (s) say while he was on the pulpit,

'Indeed, paternal cousins of Tamim Al-Dari sailed the sea....' "[70]

Women were able to see the imam when he preached, which helped maintain attentiveness and communication. Therefore, many women narrated hadith based on their studentship to the Prophet (s) and several women narrated parts of the Quran directly from the recitation of the Prophet (s).

Umm Hisham Bint al-Harith Ibn Al-Nu'man narrated:

"I memorised Surat Qaf [Chapter 50] only from the mouth of the Messenger of Allah (s) he would recite the whole chapter within his speech every Friday."[71]

Abdullah Ibn Abbas narrated:

"Umm al-Fadl heard me reciting 'Wal Mursalati Urfa' [Chapter 77]. She commented, 'O my son! By Allah, your recitation made me remember that it was the last surah I heard from Allah's Messenger, peace be upon him. He recited it in a maghrib prayer.' "[72]

Umm Salamah, the wife of Allah's Messenger (s) said:

"I used to hear people making a mention of the Water Reservoir in the next life, but I did not hear about it from Allah's Messenger. One day, while a girl was combing my hair, I heard Allah's Messenger say: 'O people.' I said to the girl: 'Let me go and hear what the Prophet (s) has to say.' She said: 'The Prophet (s) addressed men, not women.' I said: 'He addressed people and I am amongst the people.' I went and heard Allah's Messenger (s) saying: 'I shall reach the

Water Reservoir in the next life before you. Therefore, be cautious lest one of you should be driven
away like a stray camel. I would ask about the reason,
and it would be said to me: You don't know what innovations they made after you left them. So I would
also say: Stay away.' "[73]

Narrated Abu Uthman:

"I was informed that Gabriel came to the Prophet
(s) while Umm Salamah was with him. He started
talking to the Prophet (s). The Prophet (s) asked
Umm Salamah, 'Do you know who is this?' She
replied, 'Dihya Al-Kalbi.' When Gabriel left, Umm
Salamah said, 'By Allah, I did not take him for anybody other than Dihya until I heard the sermon
when the Prophet (s) informed people about the
news of Gabriel's visit.' "[74]

It was narrated from Asma bint Abu Bakr that she said:

"The sun eclipsed during the lifetime of the Prophet
(s)...then, I came and entered the Mosque, and saw
the Messenger of Allah (s) standing up (in prayer).
I joined him in prayer, and he kept standing up for
so long..."[75]

Hence, the best design of a mosque is the Prophet's design, as illustrated above and in these narrations. This design
solves all the problems that current designs cause, and helps
the Muslim community achieve so many important objectives.

Drawing lines on the ground or using low barriers could
be used to organise the areas of prayer for men, women, and

children, if needed. This could be a solution if there is a concern about confusion, disputes or overcrowding. However, it is contrary to the Prophet's Sunnah to isolate women in separate rooms, behind curtains or to prevent them from sighting the imam or listening to his speech directly. There is enough evidence to confirm that women used to see the Prophet (s) in the mosque, and that hearing him directly had a positive impact on their acquisition of knowledge and on teaching others.

~

CHAPTER 9

Is there such a thing as a "men's entrance"
to the mosque?

If the Prophetic example is our example, then the answer is no. A "women's entrance" was added to the mosque after the Prophet's time, where men were not allowed through. Otherwise, there is no evidence from the Sunnah of the Prophet (s) or his companions, that any specific entrance was ever dedicated to men, where women were not allowed through.

As previously illustrated, the Prophet (s) defined three entrances that were used by both men and women:

1. Al-Rahmah (Mercy) entrance, which is also called Atikah's door (to the west).

2. Othman's entrance, currently known as Jibril's door. This is the door through which the Prophet (s) would usually enter, since it was to the east, close to his rooms.

3. The third entrance was located at the rear to the south. At the beginning, the qibla direction was towards Jerusalem. When the qibla was shifted to the direction of the Kaba in Mecca, during the second Hijri year, the southern entrance was blocked, and a northern entrance was opened.[76]

Mosque entrances were accessible to both men and women during the lifetime of the Prophet (s) and during the time of Abu Bakr, the first caliph. Then, when the mosque became much more crowded, Omar, the second caliph, decided to assign a specific entrance for women only, and prohibited men from entering the mosque through it.

It is reported in Abu Dawud's *Sunan* that Nafi Ibn Omar said: "Omar ibn Al-Khattab said, 'It would be better if we leave this entrance for women.' " Another narration from Nafi indicated that, "Omar Ibn Al-Khattab would prevent men from entering the mosque through the women's entrance."[77]

It is important to note that women were never prevented from entering the mosque through the main entrances as there was no concept of a "men's entrance."

The issue of assigning a specific entrance for women is based on an *ijtihad* (reasoning) by Omar and is meant for practical purposes. It was not part of the original commands of Islam, and thus is subject to change with the considerations of time and place.

Today, and especially in countries with Muslim minorities, it is only appropriate for the mosque's main entrances to be open for both men and women. Adding a women's only entrance might be convenient, but women should not be restricted to using this entrance. This is a correction that is overdue for every contemporary mosque design.

What we also observe in today's mosque, in all cultures, is that women are scolded if they attempt to enter the mosque from the "men's entrances." This is a shameful and un-Islamic attitude. It is forbidden for a man to deal in a rude way with his sisters in Islam, as we unfortunately see in our present reality.

In fact, ill-treatment of Muslim women, both inside and

outside mosques, is one of the major problems besetting Muslim communities. Such an attitude makes the upcoming Muslim youth disheartened towards Islam and Muslims, and misrepresents the great message of Islam to non-Muslims.

~

CHAPTER 10

Are children allowed in the mosque?
Where do they pray?

The consistent practice during the lifetime of the Prophet (s) was that the father or mother prays while carrying the child when he/she is small. Older children would form separate rows between men and women. It was also recorded that sometimes the imam was a child, such as Amr Ibn Salamah. The hadith we referred to earlier confirmed that Amr lead the prayer at the age of seven.

Today, however, there are very few children trained to observe prayers with due concentration, let alone lead them. It is thus important to include "mosque training" in our Islamic education curricula and in our family programmes. It is also more suitable that either parent in the mosque accompany or carry the child, or to dedicate special halls for children where they can be guided by volunteering adults. This is needed especially in public occasions where there are large numbers of children inside the mosque.

It is the Sunnah of the Prophet (s) to instruct children how to pray correctly, even during the prayers offered by the teacher or parent. Ibn Abbas (r) related the following from his childhood memories:

"One night I decided to pray behind the Prophet (s) while standing to his left. In the middle of the prayer, he took me by the hand and guided me to stand to his right."[78]

Ibn Abbas also reported:

"One day, the call for the dawn prayer was announced while I was getting ready to perform two voluntary *rak'ahs*. So the Prophet (s), before he started praying, held my hand and remarked: 'Are you then praying four *rak'ahs* for the dawn prayer' "[79]

However, some Muslim communities habitually prevent children, especially females, from visiting the mosques. Such practice contradicts the teachings of the Quran and the confirmed Sunnah of the Prophet (s) as the following illustrates.

In a chapter titled, "Chapter on Carrying a Small Girl on One's Shoulder While Praying", Bukhari reported on the authority of Abu Qatadah Al-Ansari that the Prophet (s) prayed while carrying Umamah, his granddaughter. Umamah was the daughter of the Prophet's daughter, Zainab, and Abu Al-'As ibn Rabiah Ibn Abd Shams. When the Prophet (s) prostrated, he would put Umamah down, and before he stood up he would pick her up again.[80]

In a different narration, the Prophet (s) said, "I start my prayer with an intent to prolong it. But when I hear the crying of a baby I shorten it for fear that his mother might be distressed."[81]

It was also narrated that once the Prophet prostrated and his grandchildren, Al-Hasan and Al-Hussein, mounted his back. So, he spent a long time prostrating and did not push them away until they chose to climb down from his back. When asked about the reason, he replied, "My sons were riding on my back and I did not like to disturb them." And when his companions attempted to prevent his grandchildren from climbing on his back while praying, he would signal them to leave them. Afterwards, when he finished the prayer, he would carry them on his lap.[82]

This is the Sunnah of the Prophet (s) related to children in the mosque. This is the loving and compassionate model to follow.

~

CHAPTER 11

Can men and women interact in the mosque?

One of the current problematic issues in mosques that give access to women is the excessive sensitivity towards, and sometimes the strict banning of, ordinary interaction between men and women inside the mosque. Interestingly, the same groups of men and women do interact normally and with other men and women in all other contexts of social and professional life.

Referring again to the Sunnah, we find that interaction between men and women in the mosque did exist during the Prophet's time. It was a "normal" interaction that involved various religious and social affairs.

True, some violations were reported in the Sunnah, but they were viewed as individual cases and produced no change in the original rules of interaction between men and women, let alone in the architecture of the mosque itself.

The following hadiths are only a few examples of how men and women interacted in the mosque in the presence of the Prophet (s) as narrated by both male and female companions. They define what we may call a "normal" interaction between men and women in the mosque. The hadiths are clear enough and require no further elaboration.

We mentioned earlier the narration in which Asma (r) recounted:

"I asked a man sitting in front of me, "May Allah bless you, what did the Messenger (s) say concluding his sermon?' … "[83]

Abdul Rahman reported on the authority of Malik from Nafi from Ibn Omar:

"The companions would perform ablution together. Abdul Rahman said, I asked Malik, 'You mean men and women?' He replied, 'Yes'. I further asked, 'Was this during the lifetime of the Prophet, peace be upon him?' 'Yes,' he affirmed."[84]

Jabir (r) reported the following incident:

"The Prophet (s) used to stand on a tree trunk while he delivered his sermons. One day, a woman from the Ansar said to him, 'O Messenger of Allah! One of my servants is a carpenter. Shall I get him to construct a pulpit for you?' The Prophet (s) responded, 'Yes'. She complied, and the Prophet started using the pulpit. One Friday, while he was delivering a sermon standing on the pulpit, we heard a groaning sound coming out of the tree trunk. The Prophet (s) commented, 'This trunk is weeping because it misses my standing on it while praising Allah.' "[85]

Aisha (r) reported,

"How good the women of Al-Ansar are! Their bashfulness never stopped them from asking any type of question about the faith (in the mosque) and acquiring a good understanding of it."[86]

Abdullah Ibn Mas'ud (r) reported:

"Once the Prophet (s) entered the mosque accompanied by some women from Al-Ansar. He talked with them for a while, and eventually said, 'Any of you who loses three children will surely be rewarded for her patience by entering Paradise.' A woman – who was one of the most revered among them – stood up and asked, 'O Messenger of Allah! What about a woman who loses two children?' The Prophet said, 'And a woman who loses two children too.' "[87]

Asma bint Yazid (r) narrated:

"One day, the Messenger of Allah talked to us about Ad-Dhajjal (Anti-Christ), and then a woman said, 'O Messenger of Allah, how weak we would be in the face of Ad-Dhajjal!' The Prophet said, 'If he comes out while I am amongst you, I would argue with him, and if he comes out after me, then Allah will take care of every Muslim on my behalf.' "[88]

Abu Hurairah (r) narrated:

"The Messenger of Allah said, 'Perhaps a man amongst you tells what he did with his wife in their privacy, or a woman tells others what her husband did with her in their privacy?' A black woman stood up and said, 'Yes, by Allah, O Messenger of Allah, women do that, and men do that'. He said, 'Do not do that. It is like a male devil having an intimate act with a female devil on the road while everybody is watching.' "[89]

Aisha (r) narrated:

"Sa'd Ibn Muaz was wounded on the Battle of the Al-Khandaq [The Ditch] … Then, the Prophet (s) set up a tent in the mosque for Sa'd to be able to visit frequently.[90] Commenting on this particular narration, Ibn Hajar stated that: the Messenger of Allah (s) actually let Sa'd stay in Rufaydah's tent near his mosque. She was known for her skills in treating the wounded. The Prophet said, 'let Sa'd stay in her tent so that I can visit him from a close distance.' "[91]

The practice of what we call here a "normal interaction" between men and women in the mosque continued throughout the times of thriving in Islamic history. Women continued to voice their opinions freely, including correcting what the imam said.

One example is the story of Omar and the dowries. Omar ascended the Prophet's pulpit when he was caliph, and said to the people, "Why do you go to excess in women's dowries even though during the lifetime of the Prophet, the companions used to pay 400 dirhams or less in dowry? If the increase in the dowries was a sign of piety or honour in the sight of Allah, you would have not surpassed the companions in this regard. So, let me not hear that a man paid a woman a dowry of more than 400 dirhams." When he descended from the pulpit, a woman from the tribe of Quraysh (described in another narration as a flat-nosed, tall woman) intercepted him and said, "O Commander of the Believers!

Do you forbid the people to pay more than 400 dirhams as women's dowries?" He answered, "Yes". She replied, "Did you not hear what Allah said in the Quran about dowries?" He wondered, "Which verse do you mean?" She answered, *"Did you not hear Allah's saying, 'if you have given one of the women a qintar (great amount) in gifts, then do not take back from it anything. Would you take it in injustice and manifest sin?'* " (4:20). He said, "O Allah, I ask You for pardon! Everybody is more knowledgeable than Omar... The woman was right while the man erred."[92]

~

CHAPTER 12

*What happens when some people act
inappropriately in the mosque?*

The community of the companions was an outstanding one
in human history. Yet, they were not inviolable to mistakes,
unlike the Prophet (s). And the companions were not all at the
same level of faith. While some were willing to give up their
lives for the sake of Islam, others were not willing to give up an
unlawful gaze, even in the mosque.

It was reported in a number of authentic sources that
Ibn Abbas (r) reported:

"A pretty woman, who was described as one of the
most beautiful women, used to perform prayers in
the Prophet's Mosque in the women's line. Some
men used to go into the first row to avoid seeing
her, and some others used to lag behind so that they
would be in the last row. When the men in the last
row bowed, some of them would look behind in order to stare at her. They continued to do that until
Allah revealed: 'And indeed, We know those of you
who hasten forward, and indeed, We know those of
you who lag behind.' " (15:24)."[96]

Notice here that when some men did that indecent act in
the mosque, they were blamed and advised. There is no men-

tion in any narration of any kind of blame that was put on that "pretty woman," let alone women in general; contrary to what typically happens when a similar incident takes place today. Today, in the name of avoiding mischief (*fitnah*), it is women who are sent to side rooms or even kicked out of mosques. It is clear, however, that such mistakes at the time of the Prophet (s) had no impact on the rules that he set for the interaction between men and women in the mosque, let alone the design of the mosque itself.

Some argue that allowing such normal interaction will increase the chances of "temptation" between young men and women. The reality is that, in today's world, young men and women do not come to the mosque, out of all places, to get "tempted" in any wrong way. In fact, there is a real need, recognised by anyone dealing with the youth, to allow young men and women to see and get to know each other, within the rules and regulations of Sharia of course, to facilitate marriage prospects for them.

The Prophet's Sunnah does not teach us to block the means of decent interaction towards marriage, but rather to open these means. It was narrated that Al-Mughirah Ibn Shu'bah told the Prophet (s) that he proposed to marry a woman. The Prophet asked him, "Did you look at her?" He answered, "No". The Prophet said, "Look at her, for this is more likely to maintain a good relationship between you both."[94]

If temptation is feared, then the Prophetic way in handling such an issue is gentle advice. Abdullah Ibn Abbas (r) reported a story concerning his brother, Al-Fadl, with the Prophet (s) during pilgrimage:

"The Prophet (s) let Al-Fadl Ibn Abbas ride behind him on his she-camel, on the Day of Nahr [10th of Dhul-Hijja during the Pilgrimage Season]. Al-Fadl was a handsome man. Then, the Prophet stopped to answer people's questions about pilgrimage. A beautiful woman from the tribe of Khath'am came to ask Allah's Messenger. Attracted by her beauty, Al-Fadl started staring at her. The Prophet looked behind and gently turned Al-Fadl's face away from her."[95]

~

CHAPTER 13

*Is there a specific dress code for
Women in the mosque?*

The answer is no. There is no evidence in the Prophet's Sunnah to indicate any difference between women's, or men's, Islamic dress code in public, and what they should wear during prayers or when they visit the mosque.

It is true that Aisha (r) said:

"May Allah have mercy on the early immigrant women. When the verse *'they should draw their veils over their bosoms'* (24:31) was revealed, they tore their outer garments and made veils out of them... The believing women used to attend the fajr prayer with Allah's Apostle covered with their veiling sheets, and after finishing the prayer they would return to their homes."[96]

However, this Quranic instruction, for the covering of a woman's ornaments and charms, is for all public places, including mosques, *"except for what normally appears"* (24:31), as the Quran states.

When it comes to mosques, the Quranic special recommendation is to dress well and to "take adornment" when one goes to the mosque, man or woman. Allah says: *"O Children of*

Adam, take your adornment at every mosque." (7: 31)

But Islam, being the middle path, encourages believers to take a moderate position between two extremes; the extreme of no adornments whatsoever and the other extreme of taking excessive adornments. This is the balanced conclusion from studying *all* narrations related to this issue and integrating their meanings in one holistic view.

If we take one form for adornment that has to do with wearing perfumes, we will see from the collective logic of *all* narrations that the Prophet (s) encouraged the same middle path.

On the side of excess, the Prophet (s) forbade a woman to wear too much perfume or incense in public to the extent of drawing the attention of men with her intense smell or to arouse desires by her fragrance. Abu Musa Al-Ash'ari narrated that the Messenger of Allah (s) said: "If a woman puts on perfume and walks by men with an intention to make them smell her fragrance, then she is so and so."[97]

It is in this context that we understand the instructions of forbidding women from wearing perfume when they visit the mosques. Zainab, the wife of Abdullah Ibn Mas'ud, reported: "The Messenger of Allah (s) said to us: 'When any one of you comes to the mosque, she should not apply perfume.' "[98] A number of other narrations from Abu Hurairah addressed the same issue including, "any woman who has been perfumed with incense should not attend the night prayer with us,"[99] and, "The prayer of a woman who uses perfume for this mosque is not accepted,"[100] and so on.

Some scholars took these instructions to the other extreme and forbade women from wearing perfume of any kind. Ibn Hazm, the Andalusian, commented on the above narrations by stating that a woman is not allowed to go to the mosque unless she "smells bad" (*sayyi'at al-reeh*)![101] Ibn Hazm is one of the imams of the Literalist (*Zahiri*) School, and this particular comment is a textbook example of how ugly and un-Islamic a literalist understanding can be.

What Ibn Hazm and other scholars chose to ignore, in the name of literalism, is that the Prophet (s) himself recommended his female companions on a number of occasions to look and smell good, without excess of course. Here are a few examples to reflect upon.

Aisha reported that Asma asked the Prophet (s) about how to wash after finishing her period. He advised her: "Take some water and leaves from a lote-tree (*sidr*). Wash your body and hair very well with them, and rinse with water. Then use a piece of cotton with musk." Asma asked: "Where do I apply the musk?" The Prophet said, "*subhanallah!*" (glory be to Allah) and did not answer, but Aisha answered: "Where the blood was".[102]

Anas narrated that the Prophet (s) saw spittle on one of the mosque's walls, which made him quite angry. A woman from the Ansar stood up, walked to it, rubbed it off and put some perfume on the wall instead. The Prophet said: "How beautiful this is!"[103]

Aisha Bin Abdullah narrated that the Prophet (s) instructed her when they celebrate the birth of a newborn to put perfume on his/her head.[104]

And finally, Aisha, the Mother of the Believers, narrated that a woman came to the Prophet (s) with a scroll that she gave him from behind a curtain. The Prophet asked: "Is this a man's hand or a woman's hand?" She said: "A woman." He said: "If you are a woman then at least put some henna on your fingers."[105]

CHAPTER 14

Is it preferable for women to attend congregational prayers in the mosque?

Allah says in the chapter that is called "The Day of Congregation" or "Friday": *"O believers, when a call is made for prayer on the Day of Congregation, hasten to God's remembrance."* (62:9) This verse, and other verses that mentioned believers and mosques, did not differentiate between men and women.

However, it is quite established in the tradition of the Islamic jurisprudence that women, unlike men, are not required to attend the Friday prayer. Some authentic hadiths are narrated from the Prophet (s) to this effect. For example, "Women are not required to attend the Friday prayer in congregation."[106] Nevertheless, despite this unanimous agreement, it is a recommendation for women to attend the Friday congregational prayers whenever they can.[107]

Other congregational prayers are recommended for men and women alike, and there is no proof that indicates otherwise. Women are included within the general implication of the Prophet's (s) hadith,

> "Prayer in congregation is 27 times superior to the prayer offered by a person alone."[108]

Abu Hurairah (r) also narrated that the Prophet (s) said,

"The prayer offered in congregation by anyone of you is twenty-some degrees superior to the prayer offered alone in one's house or in the market. This is because when you perform ablution and do it perfectly, and go out to the mosque having no intention other than offering the prayer and motivated only by the prayer, then every step you take elevates your rank by one degree and causes one sin to be removed. And the angels will keep invoking blessing on any of you so long as you remain in the place of prayer, saying, 'O Allah, forgive him; O Allah, have mercy on him; O Allah, accept this repentance,' so long as you do not get your ablution nullified or harm anyone ... You will be reckoned as praying so long as waiting for the next prayer and did not leave the mosque."[109]

CHAPTER 15

Are non-Muslim men and women allowed in the mosque? Can they pray there?

I once heard a disturbing story from a South African convert to Islam. He told me he was interested in Islam for a long time, but when he decided to visit the nearby mosque, he was told he was not allowed inside because he was not Muslim! Finally, after a year of trying, some of his Muslim friends convinced the mosque's imam to allow him in. He liked the atmosphere in the mosque and asked if he could read the Quran, but he was told he could not as he was a non-believer and therefore not clean enough to touch the Quran! It was only with Allah's mercy and the support from mature Muslim friends that he eventually converted. Yet, years after becoming a Muslim, he still complained about the rigid leadership of this Muslim community when it came to inviting his relatives to Islam, particularly his female relatives, since Muslim women themselves were not allowed in the mosque to start with.

The above story demonstrates that some flawed ideas about the role of the mosques, the status of women, and the mission of the Quran, are still prevalent in our mosques and perpetrated by some uninformed and unqualified community leaders. The mosque is not a place that is exclusively for Muslims, the Quran is not a message that is exclusively for Muslims, and women are equally welcome to the mosque. In fact, non-Muslims, men and women, are especially invited to visit the mosque and read the Quran. Allah in the Quran called upon "all people," "People of the Book," and "disbelievers" to read the Quran, reflect upon it, and come to Muhammad (s) to ask when they have questions. Allah certainly did not forbid non-believers from reading His Message! His Message is directed to them, to start with.

Ibn Ishaq narrated in his *Seerah* (Biography of the Prophet) a story about a delegation of Christians from Najran in Yemen who visited the Prophet (s) in his mosque in Medina. The delegation debated in public with the Prophet (s) as well as with the Jews of Medina in the mosque. When their prayer was due, they prayed the Christian prayers inside the mosque after they sought the Prophet's permission to do so. The following are quotes from the narrations related to this story, which were quoted by Ibn al-Qayyim.[110] They deserve some reflection.

> "A delegation of Christians from Najran came to the Messenger of Allah in Medina and entered his mosque wearing their colourful robes and garments. That was after he had prayed the Asr prayer. They were accompanied by an entire caravan of camels led by Bani Al-Harith Ibn Ka'b. The companions of the Messenger of Allah who saw them said that they never saw a delegation like it before or after that. When their time of worship came, they stood up to perform their worship in the Prophet's Mosque. He said to his companions, 'Let them worship,' so they prayed towards the east.
>
> … Then the Christians of Najran and the Jews of Medina debated in the presence of the Prophet (s)

in the mosque. The rabbis argued that Abraham was a Jew, and the Christians argued that he was a Christian. Allah, then, revealed these verses to address them: *'People of the Book! Why do you dispute concerning Abraham? The Torah was not sent down, neither the Gospel, but after him. What, have you no reason? Verily, you are those who have disputed about that of which you have knowledge. Why do you then dispute concerning that which you have no knowledge? It is Allah Who knows, and you know not. No; Abraham in truth was not a Jew, neither a Christian; but he surrendered to Allah in peace and was pure in faith; certainly he was never of the idolaters. Surely the people who are closest to Abraham are those who followed him, and this Prophet, and those who believe in him; and God is the Protector of the believers.'* (3:65–68).

… Then, a rabbi asked: 'Do you Muhammad want us to worship you as the Christians have worshipped Jesus the Son of Mary?' And a Christian man from Najran asked: 'Is this what you are calling us for, Muhammad?' The Messenger of Allah (s) said: 'I seek refuge in Allah to worship anything but Him or order anyone to worship anything but Him. He did not send me or order me to say what you are saying. Allah revealed this Quran to be read: *"Allah would never give the Book, authority, or prophesy to any person who would tell others to be his servants instead of being the servants of Allah. He would rather tell them to be worshippers of Allah and to teach and study the Book.' " (3:79).*

Ibn Kathir in his interpretation of verse 61 in Chapter 3, added the following detail, which we mentioned earlier, about the rest of the story of the people of Najran:

> "They refused to acknowledge the truth. Then, when dawn broke, the Prophet (s), after informing them of the newly revealed verses, came out with Al-Hasan and Al-Hussain wrapped in a velvet cloth of his, and Fatimah walking behind him."[111]

We can see from the above narrations that the Prophet's Mosque was an open place of dialogue with the followers of other religions, men and women; a dialogue that was open, honest and carries no compulsion. Today's mosques should apply this model from the Prophetic example.

~

CHAPTER 16

Does menstruation prohibit women from entering mosques, reading Quran or performing tawaf?

Let me start by saying that my understanding is that the House of Allah is never "off-limits" for anyone, man or woman, at any time.

However, jurists differ concerning the "permissibility" of entering the mosque for a menstruating woman. Sheikh Yusuf Al-Qaradawi issued a fatwa in this regard in which he included a survey of various opinions. He wrote:

"Jurists have considerably different opinions regarding the staying in the mosque for a menstruating woman, or women and men in a state of ritual impurity (*janabah*), i.e. after acts of intimacy, without bathing, as Allah Almighty says,

'*O you who have believed, do not approach prayer while you are intoxicated, until you know what you are saying, or in a state of ritual impurity except those passing through a place of prayer, until you have bathed.*' (4:43)

The Hanbali jurists deemed it permissible for such a person to stay in the mosque in case he/she has performed ablution (*wudu*), drawing on the hadith narrated by Sa'id ibn Mansur and Al-Athram from Ata' Ibn Yasar that he said, 'I saw some of the companions of the Prophet (s) in a state of ritual impurity while staying in the mosque after performing ablution.' "

Other jurists, however, deemed it permissible for a menstruating woman or a woman in her postpartum period to stay in the mosque whether they have performed ablution or not, since no authentic hadith is reported to this effect. Besides, the hadith that reads, "I do not allow a menstruating woman or a ritually impure person to enter the mosque" is ranked weak. Hence, there is no solid proof prohibiting it, and thus the default ruling of permissibility remains applicable.

Imam Ahmad, Al-Muzni, Abu Dawud, Ibn Al-Mundhir and Ibn Hazm maintained this view. They all drew for evidence on the hadith narrated by Abu Hurairah and recorded in Al-Bukhari and Muslim and other hadith compilations that, 'a Muslim never becomes impure'.

They also drew on analogy between the case of a Muslim in that state and that of a non-Muslim. Since a non-Muslim is allowed to enter the mosque, regardless of their state, a Muslim is more entitled to such permissibility.

I personally incline towards this opinion given the available proofs and on our methodology of facilitation and lifting distressful hindrances for Muslims, especially for a menstruating woman.

She is more entitled to such facilitation than a person with ritual impurity, since that person is in a willingly incurred state that can be lifted by simply taking a bath whenever they wish. It is different from menstruation, which Allah has destined for females; a woman cannot lift it willingly or finish it before its due course.

Moreover, some women need to frequent the mosque in order to attend religious lessons or the like, and thus they should not be prevented access to it."[112]

The hadith quoted here by Sheikh Al-Qaradawi, "I do not allow a menstruating woman or a person with ritual impurity to enter the mosque" is not weak. It is part of an authentic hadith narrated by Abu Dawud, and others, through a chain of narrators from Jasrah bint Dijajah. She said:

"I heard Aisha, may Allah be pleased with her, say, The Messenger of Allah came and saw that the doors of the houses of his companions were facing the mosque. He said, 'Turn the direction of the doors away from the mosque.' The Prophet then entered and the people did not take any step in this regard hoping that some concession might be revealed. He came upon them again and said, 'Turn the direction of these doors from the mosque; I do not permit a menstruating woman or a person with ritual impurity to enter the mosque.' "[113]

However, there is another sound narration that added the phrase, "except for Muhammad and the household of Muhammad,"[114] which means that it was not a ritual rule related to menstruation, but rather a matter of organisation.

In addition, we referred above to the hadith narrated by Aisha (r) about the young lady who came to the Prophet and embraced Islam and lived in a tent in the mosque.[115] Explaining how this hadith implies the permissibility of staying in the mosque for a menstruating woman, Ibn Hazm stated:

> "This was a woman residing in the mosque of the Prophet (s) and as a woman, she normally has menses. Yet, the Prophet did not prevent her from staying there. Something that is not banned by the Prophet is lawful."[116]

As for reciting the Quran by a menstruating woman or a person with a ritual impurity, there is no evidence for those who make it unlawful. The following is Ibn Taymiyyah's confirmation of this fact:

> "The only hadith here is narrated from Isma'il ibn Ayyash from Musa ibn Uqbah from Nafi' from Ibn Omar that he said, 'Neither a menstruating woman nor a person who is ritually impure should recite anything from the Quran.' However, this hadith, reported by Abu Dawud and others, is graded as weak according to the unanimous agreement of hadith scholars. Ibn Ayyash's reports from the Hijaz narrators are weak, unlike his reports from the Levantine narrators. Moreover, no trustworthy scholar reported this narration from Nafi' himself.

> In addition, it is well known that, during the lifetime of the Prophet, when women had their menses, the Prophet would not forbid them to recite the Quran,

just as he would not forbid them to recite invocations. Rather, he ordered the menstruating women to go out on the Eid day and to recite *takbir* along with the rest of the Muslims.

He also ordered a menstruating woman to observe all the Hajj rituals with the exception of circumambulating the Kaba, and hence women would normally perform the rituals in Muzdalifah, Mina, and other places.[117]

It is interesting that the followers of Ibn Taymiyyah today, from the Salafi school, do not take his own opinion on this issue, and cause women a lot of distress because of this restriction, especially when women visit the Sacred Mosque in Mecca and the Prophet's Mosque in Medina.

Another question comes up every season of pilgrimage about the permissibility of a woman to circumambulate the Kaba (*tawaf*) during pilgrimage while she has her menses. The problem lies in the impossibility of a menstruating woman to stay in Mecca, if she is not a citizen of the Gulf countries, until her period ends, as one opinion implies. It is also impossible for most women to return later to perform *tawaf* at a later date, as the other opinion dictates. Today, these two solutions require obtaining necessary visas and passing through other numerous costly procedures.

The issue is extensively discussed by Ibn Al-Qayyim in his famous book, *I'lam Al-Muwaqqi'in* (Information for the Muftis). The following is an excerpt:

"The Prophet (s) forbade menstruating women to circumambulate the Kaba until the period ends, and said to the woman having menses, 'Do what a pilgrim does except that you should not circumambulate the Kaba.' Therefore, some people thought that this is a general ruling that applies at all times and in all cases, without discrimination between the cases of ability and inability to do so, or between the times of possibility and impossibility to stay in Mecca until the end of a woman's period to perform tawaf.

Some scholars adhered to the literal meaning of the text, and deemed *tawaf* impermissible during menstruation just like prayer and fasting. They maintain that the prohibition related to these three acts of worship is identical and, therefore, forbiddance of tawaf during menstruation is as same as the forbiddance of praying then.

However, another two groups of scholars argue against this opinion, and the first of the two held that tawaf performed by a woman during her menses is valid and that menstruation does not render tawaf impermissible. They argued that although ritual purity is required for tawaf, menstrual bleeding does not invalidate tawaf but only necessitates offering a sacrificial animal to make up for it. But tawaf itself is still valid. This opinion is held by Abu Hanifah and his companions, and by Ahmad...

The other group deemed the necessity of ritual purity for *tawaf* similar to all the conditions of prayer that are obligatory with ability and that are dropped in case of inability. They further argue that ritual purity is not more binding for tawaf than it is for prayer, and if it is dropped due to inability in case of prayer, then it is more entitled to be dropped in case of inability during tawaf ...

Almighty Allah said, '*So fear Allah as much as you are able*' (64:16) and the Prophet (s) said, 'When I command you to do something, then do as much of it as you can.' Hence, a woman going through this situation has no option other than this, i.e. doing tawaf while she is in menses. If she does so then she fulfills as much of the obligation as she can. According to the Sharia texts and rules, nothing else becomes binding on her."[118]

At the present time, some women adopt the fatwa that allows using hormone pills to delay their period despite the high potential of adverse health effects. There is no need for that. They should do their tawaf despite their menses. Facilitation is the proper approach and the correct understanding of the Sunnah.

CHAPTER 17

Are there limits on women's participation in the mosque's social activities?

The answer is no. Women participated in a number of social activities during the time of the Prophet (s). The following are examples, some of which were quoted earlier in various contexts:

Al-Rubayyi' Bint Mu'awwidh Ibn Afra' (r), said that the Messenger of Allah (s) sent a person on the morning of Ashura to the villages of Ansar around Medina with this message:

> "He who got up in the morning fasting he should complete his fast, and he who had had his breakfast in the morning, he should complete the rest of the day in fasting." So, we henceforth observed the fast on it and, God willing, made our children observe that. We used to go to the mosque and make toys out of wool for the children so that when they felt hungry and wept for food we gave them these toys to distract them, till it was time to break the fast.[119]

Aisha (r) narrated, as was mentioned earlier:

> "Sa'd Ibn Muaz was wounded on the Battle of the Al-Khandaq (The Ditch) ... Then, the Prophet (s) set up a tent in the mosque for Sa'd to be able to visit fre-

quently."[120] Commenting on this particular narration, Ibn Hajar stated that: "The Messenger of Allah (s) actually let Sa'd stay in Rufaydah's tent near his mosque. She was known for her skills in treating the wounded. The Prophet said, 'let Sa'd stay in her tent so that I can visit him from a close distance.' "[121]

Jabir (r) reported the following incident:

The Prophet (s) used to stand on a tree trunk while he delivered his sermons. One day, a woman from the Ansar said to him, 'O Messenger of Allah! One of my servants is a carpenter. Shall I get him to construct a pulpit for you?' The Prophet (s) responded, 'Yes'. She did, and the Prophet started using the pulpit. One Friday, while he was delivering a sermon standing on the pulpit, we heard a groaning sound coming out of the tree trunk. The Prophet (s) commented, 'This trunk is weeping because it misses my standing on it while praising Allah.' "[122]

Bukhari and Muslim narrated after Aisha as well:

"Allah's Apostle invited me on a day of Eid to watch the Abyssinians who were playing in the mosque, displaying their skill with spears. He asked: 'Would you like to watch?' I answered: 'Yes'. So I stood behind him and he lowered his shoulder so I can put my chin on it. I did and leaned with my face on his cheek and watched. Eventually, he asked me several times if I wanted to leave and I replied every time: 'Please wait'. I was not interested in watching, really, but on that day I wanted women especially to know my status with him. Therefore, appreciate a young lady's keenness to be playful."[123]

We also cited earlier that Jabir Ibn Abdullah (r) reported, according to Bukhari:

"I attended Eid Prayer with the Messenger of Allah. He started with the prayer before the sermon, without an *adhan* or an *iqamah*. Then, he stood up, and while leaning on Bilal, commanded people to fear Allah and obey His commands. He started with the men and advised them, and then walked towards the women and advised them. He said: 'Give charity'... Women started giving out their jewellery in charity, throwing their earrings and rings in Bilal's garment.[124]

It is to be noted, in the context of charity, that women today donate a great deal to mosques and their activities. It is unfair and un-Islamic that they donate for an organisation that does not give them equal access or proper service.

Abu Hurairah narrated that a black woman, who used to clean the mosque, passed away. When the Messenger (s) asked about her, they informed him that she had died. He then said, "Why did you not inform me when she died? Guide me to her grave." So, he approached her grave and offered the funeral prayer for her there.[125]

Anas narrated that the Prophet (s) saw a spittle on one of the mosque's walls, which made him quite angry. A woman from the Ansar stood up and walked to it, rubbed it off and put some perfume on the wall instead. The Prophet said: "How beautiful this is!"[126]

The above examples illustrate that women's contribution to the social role of the Prophet's Mosque was invaluable. It is of ultimate importance to revive this contribution today.

There is also ample evidence from the time of the Prophet (s) to allow *i'tikaf* (staying in the mosque) during Ramadan and in other months. Aisha (r) reported: "The Prophet (s) used to perform i'tikaf during the last ten days of Ramadan until he passed away; his wives followed this practice after him."[127]

Aisha also reported that the Prophet (s) used to practise i'tikaf in the last ten days of Ramadan and she used to pitch a tent for him; he would enter it after offering the fajr prayer. Hafsa (r) asked the permission of Aisha to pitch a tent for herself and Aisha allowed her. So, Hafsa pitched her tent. When Zainab bint Jahsh (r) saw it, she pitched another tent. In the morning the Prophet (s) noticed the tents. He commented, "Do you think that they intended to do righteousness by doing this?"[128] So, he abandoned i'tikaf in that month and observed it later in the month of Shawwal for ten days.[129]

Safiyah bint Huyai (r), wife of the Prophet (s) narrated that she visited the Messenger (s) while he was staying in the mosque to observe i'tikaf during the last ten nights of the month of Ramadan. She spoke to him for a while and then she got up to return home. The Prophet (s) got up to accompany her. When they reached the gate of the mosque, two Ansari men passed by. They greeted the Messenger and quickly went ahead. The Prophet said to them, "Do not be in a hurry, She is Safiyah bint Huyai." They exclaimed, "Glory be to Allah."[130]

~

CHAPTER 18

Can women lecture men in the mosque?

During his lifetime, the Prophet (s) used to teach and instruct people in his mosque. His companions followed suit after he passed away. Although there are no reports of women, or men, systematically teaching in the mosque during the Prophetic era, there are tens of thousands of prophetic traditions that were transmitted by women over the early centuries. Female companions, especially the Prophet's wives, were amongst the highest authorities in the Prophet's Sunnah.

As a matter of fact, one of the features of scholarship following the Prophet's time was that male scholars of hadith used to learn hadith reports from female companions and their students.

In her excellent book, *Women's Role in Serving Hadith During the First Three Decades*, Amal Qurdash named a number of female hadith narrators who taught great male hadith scholars including Fatimah, daughter of Imam Malik Ibn Anas, Khadijah Umm Muhammad, Zainab Bint Sulaiman al-Hashimiyah, Zainab Bint Sulaiman Ibn Abu Ja'far Al-Mansur, Umm Omar al-Thaqafiyah, Asma Bint Asad Ibn Al-Furat, Sulaiha Bint Abu Na'im, Samanah Bint Hamdan al-Anbaiyah and Abdah Bint Abdulrahman Ibn Mus'ab.

Qurdash counted the numbers of female companions

from whom great imams narrated hadith as follows:

- Al-Bukhari narrated hadith from 31 female companions in his *Al-Jami*.

- Muslim narrated from 36 female companions in his *Al-Jami*.

- Abu Dawud, in his *Sunan*, narrated from 75 female companions.

- Al-Tirmidhi narrated from 46 female companions in his *Sunan*.

- Al-Nasa'i narrated from 65 female companions in his *Sunan*.

- And Ibn Majah, in his *Sunan* as well, narrated from 60 female companions.

She adds,

"It is only after the death of all the wives of the Prophet (s) that narrating hadith from women declined. The wives of the Prophet were frequently visited and referred to by female scholars. However, transmitting hadith by women continued, yet less frequently, until all junior companions, who lived long like Anas, Abdullah Ibn Abu Awfa and Ibn Omar, passed away."[131]

This decrease, observed by the researcher, is actually associated with the decline of Islamic civilisation itself. It is also obviously connected with the practice of barring women from going to the mosque in many places.

Yet, the information we have about female Muslim scholars during that golden era reveals the important role that can be played by Muslim women when they engage in the fields of knowledge and education.

In a research of historic importance, Dr Mohammad Akram Nadwi compiled information on the female narrators of hadith (*Al-Muhaddithat*) and analysed their invaluable contribution to what we know about Islam today. The preface, the first volume of a 40-volume biographical dictionary, was published separately in English.[132] Detailed studies of this work are necessary to draw a full picture of female scholarship along the Islamic history and across the world. However, in relation to the question we are dealing with in this chapter, I will quote one paragraph below related to the role of women scholars as teachers:

> "The women who had knowledge of the religion transmitted that knowledge to men as well as women. Indeed, given that the majority of students of hadith were men, we would expect the majority of the women's students to have been men. Their numbers varied in different periods, but in some periods were very high: for example, al-Dhahabi in his account of Hafiz Abu Abdillah Muhammad ibn Mahmud ibn al-Najjar (d. 643) reports from Ibn al-Sa'ati that '[Ibn al-Najjar's] teachers included 3000 men and 400 women.' It should suffice as evidence of the authority of women in preserving and transmitting the Sunnah of God's Messenger that some of the greatest of his Companions and, after them, some of the greatest imams and jurists in the history of Islamic scholarship relied on women teachers.[133]

To answer our question about women and teaching in the

mosque, there is no proof that women should not be permitted to teach men and women in the mosque. To the contrary, history shows that women's role in Islamic scholarship, especially in the mosques, marked a thriving Islamic civilisation and flourishing scholarship in all fields of Islamic knowledge. The mosque should return to take a central role in the revival of the Islamic knowledge in our time.

CHAPTER 19

Can women lead congregational prayers?
Can they perform the call for prayers?

There is no dispute that women could lead other women in congregational prayers, Al-Shafi'i, Ibn Abu Shaibah and Abdul-Razzaq, among others, reported that Umm Salamah, the Mother of the Believers (r) led other women in prayers while standing among them in the same row.

Muhammad Ibn Al-Husain also reported from Ibrahim An-Nakh'i that Aisha (r) used to lead women in prayer during the month of Ramadan standing among them in the same row.[143] Al-Hakim reported in his *Mustadrak* that the Mother of Believers, Aisha (r) used to call the *adhan* and *iqamah* and then lead women in prayers.[135]

Despite the authenticity of these narrations and the practice of the Mothers of the Believers (r), I was surprised to find out that many major scholars were actually hesitant to allow women to lead other women in prayers! For example, Ibn Qudamah writes:

> "There are two different opinions regarding whether it is desirable for a woman to lead other women in congregational prayer. One reported opinion is that it is recommended. Aisha, Umm Salamah, Ata', Al-Thawri, Al-Awza'i, Al-Shafi'i, Ishaq, and Abu

Thawr are of the opinion that a woman can lead other women in prayer. On the other hand, it is narrated
that Ahmad Ibn Hanbal (may Allah be merciful to
him) did not recommend it. The Hanafi scholars also
regarded it undesirable, but if such congregational
prayer is done, it will still be valid. Furthermore, Al-
Sha'bi, Al-Nakh'i and Qatadah maintain that women
are permitted to perform prayer this way in super-
erogatory prayers but not in obligatory ones".[136]

It is interesting that these scholars were distracted from
the above authentic narrations with some whimsical opinions
or narrations that are at the weakest level of authenticity. It
is reported that Jabir ibn Abdullah (r) said: "The Prophet (s)
addressed us in a speech and stated, 'A woman may not lead
a man in prayer.' Another version of the hadith: 'A man may
not be led by a woman in prayer, nor may a *muhajjir* (a believer who migrated to Medina) be led by a Bedouin, nor may a
committed believer be led by a corrupt person unless one is
coerced by a ruler and fears his sword or whip.' "[137]

Another weak hadith was reported by Ibn Abi Shaibah
in his *Musanaf* from Abu Bakr quoting Waki' from ibn Abi
Zi'b from a freed slave of Bani Hashim from Ali that he said:
"Women should not lead prayers."[138]

However, these three narrations, despite being popular in
the scholarly and social contexts, are "weak" and there is is
obvious lying within their wordings.

It is to be noted here that the popular saying, "Move
them back to the rear designated for them by Allah" is not a
hadith and cannot be used to corroborate any argument in
this question. Rather, it is a saying reported in *Al-Muwatta'*

from Abdullah Ibn Mas'ud, the companion (r).[139]

In the *Musannaf* of Abdul-Razzaq, Ibn Mas'ud reportedly said:

> "Women and men of the children of Israel used to pray together. Some women would wear high wooden shoes to get taller so their lovers can identify them. Thus, they were afflicted with menstruation. Therefore, move women back to the rear as this is the place designated for them by Allah."[140]

It is clear and interesting that Ibn Mas'ud, if the narration is true, copied this command of "move women back" from somewhere in the tradition of the Children of Israel. In Islam, women are not "punished" by menstruation, as mentioned in some biblical sources, and they are not supposed to be pushed back because some other women were involved in some sins. In Islam, *"no soul shall carry the burden of another"*. (6:164)

In fact, there is an authentic hadith from the time of the Prophet (s) in which one of the female companions led women and men in congregational prayers. The following is an analysis of the hadith and its implication.

Uthman Ibn Abu Shaibah narrated from Wakee' Ibn Al-Jarrah, from Al-Walid Ibn Abdullah Ibn Jumai', from his grandmother, from Abdul-Rahman Ibn Khallad Al-Ansari, from Um Waraqah Al-Ansariyyah:

> "When the Prophet (s) proceeded for the Battle of Badr, I said to him: 'O Prophet of Allah, allow me to accompany you in the battle; I shall nurse the patients and hopefully Allah will grant me martyrdom.' He said: 'Stay at your home; Allah, the Almighty,

will bestow martyrdom upon you.' The narrator said: 'Hence she was called the martyr. She memorised the whole Quran and sought permission from the Prophet (s) to have a *mu'adhin* (a caller to prayer) in the mosque that she had in her house. The Prophet granted her request. Abdul-Rahman Ibn Khallad [the reporter of this hadith] said, 'I did see her mu'adhin who was a very old man.' "

The hadith was narrated by Abu Dawud, with no reservations, and it is ranked *hasan* (sound) by Al-Albani.[141]

Hadith scholars disagreed about the authenticity of this hadith, despite the status of Umm Waraqah herself. Umm Waraqah (r) was one of the companions who transmitted the recitation of the Quran before it was recorded in writing. She could do so because she had memorised the entire corpus.[142]

Al-Arna'ut, for example, cited that, "The reporters' chain (*isnad*) of the hadith is weak because Abdul-Rahman Ibn Khallad and the grandmother of Al-Walid ibn Abdullah Ibn Jumai', Laila Bint Malik, are unknown."

However, with all respect to Sheikh Al-Arna'ut's scholarship, these narrators are not unknown. In fact, the hadith was narrated through different chains of reporters up to Al-Walid Ibn Abdullah Ibn Jumai' by: Ibn Sa'd in *At-Tabaqat* (both the long and short versions of the hadith) 8/457, Ibn Abi Shaibah 12/527-528, Ahmad 27282, Ibn Abi Asim in *Al-Ahad wal Mathani* 3366 and 3367, Al-Tabarani 25/326-327, Al-Hakim 1203, Al-Baihaqi in *al-Sunan* 1/406 and 3/130 and *Al-Dala'il* 6/381.

In addition, Al-Hakim narrated the same hadith, according to Bukhari and Muslim criteria, in his *Mustdarak* with the following wordings: "and the Prophet told her to lead the people of her house in the obligatory prayers."

Abu Dawud said, "I do not know a hadith having a full, connected isnad in this question other than this hadith. Indeed, Imam Muslim has already cited Al-Walid ibn Jumai' as a reliable reference."[143]

Furthermore, Ibn Khuzaimah narrated this hadith in his *Sahih*, and Al-Albani ranked it as sound (*hasan*).[144]

Ibn Hibban also listed Abdul-Rahman Ibn Khallad and Al-Walid Ibn Jumai' as credible in his *Al-Thiqat* (*The Trustworthy*).[145]

Commenting on this report Al-San'ani says in his *Subul Al-Salam*:

> "This hadith proves the validity of the woman's leading her household in prayer, even if the congregation includes males because Umm Waraqah had a mu'adhin, an aged male who called people for prayers, as mentioned in the hadith. Apparently she led him and her male and female servants. Scholars holding this opinion include Abu Thawr, Al-Muzani and Al-Tabari. The majority of scholars, however, do not support this view."[146]

Ibn Taymiyyah also supported women leading men in prayers, and rejected Ibn Hazm's claim that there is consensus among scholars on the prohibition of women's leading men in prayers altogether. Ibn Taymiyah wrote:

> "A learned woman leading unlettered men in the night prayers of Ramadan is permissible according to the famous opinion from Ahmad. As for all other congregational prayers, there are two different

opinions that Ahmad gave."[147]

He also wrote,

"The famous opinion of Ahmad is the permissibility of a woman's leading men in prayer when the need arises, such as when she is a reciter of the Quran while men are not. Thus, she can lead them in the *tarawih* prayer, since the Prophet (s) allowed Umm Waraqah to lead her household in prayer and appointed a mu'adhin to call for prayers for her."[148]

In *Al-Moghni*, Ibn Qudamah said,

"Some of our companions argue that a woman can lead men in prayers and that she prays behind them based on the report of Umm Waraqah bint 'Abdullah ibn Al-Harith that the Messenger of Allah appointed a mu'adhin for her and told her to lead her household, which includes both men and women. Our opinion against this is supported by the Prophet's hadith: 'A woman may not lead a man in prayer'. In addition, a woman cannot call adhan for men, and by the same token, she cannot lead them in prayer."[149]

The weakness of the hadith cited as evidence by Ibn Qudamah has been shown above. However, the case of a woman leading men in prayers was reported only in relation to the house mosques and prayer areas; there are no reports of women doing so in the grand mosques (*al-masjid al-jami'*).

Keeping all of the above in mind, and based on where the Islamic subcultures stand today, the opinion I choose on this issue is to restrict the women leading men in prayers to house mosques and family settings. It is more appropriate if a female in a family recites the Quran perfectly, while the rest do not, that she leads the prayers.

Scholars who allowed women to lead the prayers differed on whether she should stand in front of the men or behind them. There is no definite account from the Prophet's tradition about this issue, and the Umm Waraqah narrations did not give us this detail. The most popular opinion here is Imam Ahmad's, which Ibn Taymiyyah, again, cited in his *Fatawa*, that she stands behind them since it is more dignifying for her (*astar laha*).[150]

Regarding the call to prayer, Al-Hakim narrated from Ataa that Aisha, the Mother of the Believers, used to call the adhan and iqamah, and lead women in prayer while standing in the middle of them.[151]

Some scholars, however, prohibited women from calling the adhan and the iqamah, based on a hadith narrated from Asma bint Abi Bakr that the Prophet said, "It is not incumbent on women to call to the prayer, to announce the prayer's start, to observe Friday prayer or to have the Friday bath. And no woman should stand in front of them but rather stand in the middle of them." However, Ibn Ma'in said that the narrator of this narration, Al-Hakam Ibn Abdullah Ibn Sa'd, is not credible nor is he trustworthy. In fact, Al-Bukahri described him as "abandoned" (*matruk*), Al-Nasa'i said that his reports are shunned, and Ibn Al-Mubarak deemed him "weak." Ibn Al-Jawzi summarised these opinions and rejected that narration.[152]

~

CHAPTER 20

Can women serve on the mosque's board?
Is women's leadership forbidden by hadith?

Wherever I meet Muslim students in universities, east or west, I am asked whether female students could be elected to the board or to the presidency of their "Muslim Student Associations". It is a fact in today's world that Muslim female students everywhere are generally more active than Muslim male students, and it is quite surprising that they are not allowed leadership positions in their student organisations simply because they are not male, and often based on some strange fatwa from mediocre "scholars".

And wherever I meet with board members of mosque organisations, especially in the West, I hear complaints from members of the community that women are not allowed on the board only because they are females. Again, Muslim women are very active and carry the burden of representing Islam itself in the public sphere, in community leadership and in fundraising, more than Muslim men, especially in the West. However, in many mosque organizations, women are not allowed on the organisational board of the very community that they represent, lead, donate to, and serve!

One hadith narration is usually cited in this context, which has had quite a negative impact on the perception of women's leadership in the Muslim mind over the centuries. It is the narration by Abu Bakrah Nufai' Ibn Al-Harith Al-Thaqafi who said:

> "Allah benefited me with something I heard from the Prophet (s) during the Battle of the Camel. I almost joined the People of the Camel to fight on their side, but then I remembered what I heard from the Prophet (s) when he was told that the Persians appointed their deceased king's daughter as their queen. The Prophet said: 'A people who appoint a woman leader will never be successful.' "[153]

This is, therefore, the final narration in this book that will require some critical analysis. The above narration, like all the other previous narrations, has a context that is crucial for a proper understanding of its meaning and assessment of its narrators. The context of this narration is twofold:

1. The context in which the narrator himself, Abu Bakrah Al-Thaqafi, cited the narration.

2. The context in which the Prophet himself (s) said what he said.

Abu Bakrah Al-Thaqafi was one of the "companions," in the sense that he saw the Prophet (s). However, the story of him accusing Al-Mughirah of adultery and not producing three other witnesses is well known.[154] The Quran states: *"And those who accuse chaste women, and do not produce four witnesses, flog them with eighty stripes, and reject their testimony forever, they indeed are the fasiqun (liars, rebellious, disobedient)."* (24:4) Therefore, Omar the caliph, applied this punishment on Abu Bakrah when he refused to change his accusation and his testimony in courts was invalidated afterwards.

The context in which Abu Bakrah Al-Thaqafi recalled the hadith is interesting. He did not narrate the hadith anywhere or to anybody we know until approximately 25 years after he claimed to have heard it. The context was the Battle of the Camel, or the civil war that the companions fought in the aftermath of the assassination of the third caliph Othman in the Year 36 Hijri. Abu Bakrah Al-Thaqafi was not sure which side to take, as he said in his story, and decided finally to join the side of Ali Ibn Abu Talib (r) based on this hadith. He referred to the other side of Mu'awiyah Ibn Abu Sufyan and Aisha, the Mother of the Believers, as the "unsuccessful side" because of the leadership role that Aisha took in that battle. Aisha (r) actually led the army on her camel, which is the reason the whole battle was called the Battle of the Camel.

I believe that the political context of the narration is enough reason to reject it, whether Abu Bakrah Al-Thaqafi was a "trustworthy companion" or not. I witnessed numerous situations throughout my life where it is clear that scholars take political sides, especially if there is violence or war involved, which affect their sound judgement and perception of their rivals.

However, even if Abu Bakrah Al-Thaqafi was a trustworthy narrator, as many scholars of hadith insisted, the context of the saying of the Prophet (s) is also worth reflecting upon. The story was the news of the assassination of another king of Persia and not finding any more males in the family to take over the throne. Therefore, the king's daughter, who was a teenager, took over in a final attempt to save the kingdom that was already failing with internal disputes.

Note also that the previous King of Persia ripped the scroll that the Prophet (s) sent, and ordered two Yemenis to arrest the Prophet and bring him to Persia. When the two Yemenis arrived in Medina, the story goes that the Prophet (s) told them that Allah told him their king was killed that same morning. The Prophet, therefore, sent another message to the new king and invited him to embrace Islam. This is the context in which the Prophet (s) said that the Persians would never be successful under the leadership of their new queen – not because she is a female but because of the continuous killing of the kings and princes and their rejection of the Prophet's message.

It is very important, from a methodological point of view, to put the hadith narrations within the context of the Quranic scripts that address the same issues. The Quran does present several women as "examples," and the most obvious example in this context is the Queen of Sheba's leadership, which was indeed a successful leadership. The Quran states (excerpts from: 27:29–44):

> "When the Queen had read Solomon's letter, she said: 'O you nobles! A truly distinguished letter has been conveyed unto me. Behold, it is from Solomon, and it says, "In the name of God, The Most Gracious, The Dispenser of Grace: God says: Exalt not yourselves against Me, but come unto Me in willing surrender!' " She added: 'O you nobles! Give me your opinion on the problem with which I am now faced; I would never make a weighty decision unless you are present with me.' They answered: ' "We are endowed with power and with mighty prowess in war -- but the command is yours; consider, then, what you would command.' She said: 'Verily, whenever kings enter a country they

corrupt it, and turn the noblest of its people into the most abject. And this is the way they always behave. Hence, behold, I am going to send a gift to those people, and await whatever answer the envoys bring back.'

…Solomon said to his nobles: ' "She has arrived at the truth without any help from us, although it is we who have been given divine knowledge before her, and have long ago surrendered ourselves unto God!'

…Cried she: 'O my Sustainer! I have been sinning against myself, but now I have surrendered myself, with Solomon, unto the Sustainer of all the worlds!' "

Other than the prophets, the Queen of Sheba is the only good example of a political leader given in the Quran. It gives us the details of her expertise: skillfully consulting her ministers and respecting their opinions, their reverence of her and their willingness to commit to war or peace under her leadership, her personal intelligence and knowledge of history and geography, and her integrity and honesty in accepting the truth wherever it lies. Thus, the leadership of the Queen of Sheba is much more "Islamic" than the leadership of most Muslim male political leaders, past and present.

~

IN SUMMARY

The following is a summary of the main points that were made throughout this book.

- There is an international phenomenon of decline in mosque attendance, and women, if they are allowed to attend, are treated as "second class citizens".

- The more women-friendly the mosque is, the more likely it is to provide community services, interfaith sessions, and involve children and youth.

- Women-only mosques are a temporary solution and a way to protest women's marginalisation in today's mosques, but in the longer term they would serve to divide our communities even further.

- Given the status of women in the mosque, non-Muslims are not to be blamed when they believe misconceptions about Islam as a religion that does not welcome women and does not treat them with full dignity.

- Before dealing with any topic from an "Islamic" perspective, we should define what we mean by the very term. The true reference to what is "Islamic" is nothing other than the Word of God, the Quran, and the example or Sunnah of His Prophet (s), who was a living illustration of the Quran.

- The Quran and Sunnah contain numerous commands that prohibit "blind following" of others, including jurists and schools of Islamic law.

- The Quran and the Prophetic example are not "cultural products" as is human speech or literature. The Quran and Sunnah are revealed knowledge suitable for every place and time and are not subject to "historicisation".

- There are dozens of Quranic verses related to mosques, all of which urge all believers who seek guidance, light and knowledge, males and females alike, to frequent mosques.

- The Quran clearly forbids preventing people, male or female, from frequenting the mosques.

- The Sunnah of the Prophet (s) includes hundreds of authentic narrations indicating women's normal presence in the mosque at all times and on all occasions at the time of the Prophet (s).

- In today's context, restrictions hindering women from visiting the mosque should be removed, and instead women should be encouraged to go to the mosque and participate in its activities.

- When the Prophet (s) advised Umm Humaid to pray

at home, he was only resolving the marital disagreement between her and her husband about her praying in the mosque. Evidence is against the claims that the Prophet (s) meant for that advice to be for everybody else.

- The narrations claiming that, "a woman should see no man and that no man should see her", "a man's prayer is interrupted by a woman, a dog or a donkey, when they pass in front of a praying person", "your bad omen is in your house and your woman", and "women are the majority of the dwellers of hell" – are all non-reliable narrations.

- The Prophet's Mosque had entrances that were open for men and women alike, and had no barriers, curtains or partitions, despite their availability.

- The established Sunnah throughout the Prophet's (s) life was that men formed rows right behind the Prophet (s) starting from the first row behind him. Women's rows started at the rear of the mosque and were added forward. Children lined up in rows between the men's and women's rows.

- Women should be able to see the imam when he preaches, which helps maintain attentiveness and communication.

- Special "women's entrances" were added to the mosque after the Prophet's time, and there is no evidence from the Sunnah of the Prophet (s) or his companions, that any specific entrance was ever dedicated to men, where women were not allowed to pass through.

- The Prophet (s) used to carry children while praying and instruct them how to pray correctly, even during the prayers.

- Preventing children, especially females, from visiting the mosques contradicts the teachings of the Quran and the confirmed Sunnah of the Prophet (s).

- Normal interaction between men and women in the mosque did exist during the Prophet's time, and involved various religious and social affairs.

- When some men misbehaved in the Prophet's Mosque, they were blamed and advised. There is no mention in any narration of any blame that was put on the women involved, and no impact on the rules or the design of the mosque.

- There is no evidence in the Prophet's Sunnah to indicate any difference between women's, or men's, Islamic dress code in public, and what they should wear during prayers or when they visit the mosque.

- The Prophet (s) himself recommended his female companions on a number of occasions to look and smell good, without excess of course.

- Despite unanimous agreement that attending the Friday prayers is not required from women, it is recommended for women to attend the Friday prayers whenever they can.

- Allah certainly did not forbid non-believers from touching the Quran or reading His Message. The Quran is directed to them, to start with.

- The Prophet's Mosque was an open place for dialogue with the followers of other religions, men and women.

- A menstruating woman or a person with a ritual impurity is not forbidden from visiting the mosque or reading the Quran.

- Menstruating woman during Hajj who cannot stay beyond the season of Hajj or return for the final tawaf, are allowed to make tawaf.

- Women participated in all of the mosque's social activities during the time of the Prophet (s).

- It is unfair and un-Islamic that women donate to a mosque that does not give them equal access or proper service.

- There is ample evidence from the time of the Prophet (s) to allow women to perform i'tikaf (staying in the mosque) during Ramadan and in other months.

- One of the features of scholarship following the Prophet's time was that male scholars of hadith used to learn hadith reports from female companions and their male and female students.

- History shows that women's role in Islamic scholarship, especially in the mosques, marked a thriving Islamic civilisation and flourishing scholarship in all fields of knowledge.

- There is no dispute that women could lead other women in congregational prayers, and there are differences of opinion about women leading men in prayers. I choose the opinion that restricts the women leading men in prayers to house mosques and family settings.

- The Queen of Sheba is the only good example of political leaders, others than prophets, that is given in the Quran.

- There are no restrictions on women's leadership in Islam.

CONCLUSION

If "feminism" is a call for the dignity and rights of women, then Islam should be considered the first feminist movement in human history. The female companions of the Prophet (s) actively participated in the mosque's activities, traded in the local and regional markets, learnt and taught Quran, narrated prophetic traditions, gave fatwas, raised charity, chose their husbands, assumed various leadership roles, and fought in the battlefields when they wished to. However, after Islam's golden age, the Islamic sub-cultures deviated from the prophetic model of treating women with dignity and fairness, and many Muslim societies went back to their days of ignorance (*jahiliyah*). This book is a call to revive the Islamic ideal, starting with women reclaiming their status and role in the mosque.

Islam will take a very different path in the world when women return to the mosque and assume their primary role in all of its activities. However, the details of the issues discussed in this book prove that in order for this to happen, we have to clear a number of landmines from the field of *fiqh*. We have inherited a number of misinterpretations that shaped the perceptions about women and their roles in public life in general, and in the mosque in particular. Correcting these misinterpretations is a key remedy for many of the Muslims' social ailments today.

However, I do not believe that reviving women's roles in the mosque is possible without the women themselves struggling to achieve it. Women should not rely on men who believe in women's rights to give them their rights. These men are few and far between, and usually do not comprise a majority in fatwa councils and decision making circles for Muslim public affairs on all levels and in all regions. Therefore, women should rather form their own civil movements in order to demand their rights.

A few months ago, I was impressed by a group of South African ladies who were prevented from attending one of my lectures in a Durban mosque. My appeals to the young men who prevented them were not as effective as when the ladies themselves gathered at the front door of the mosque and insisted on entering. They eventually entered the main hall, prayed, attended the lecture, and asked questions. They set a precedent and broke the unfair barriers. This is the way to go. This is how change will happen, *insha Allah*.

NOTES

1. The book was first published in Arabic by the Egyptian Dar El-Shurouk and the Algerian Dar Al-Intifada in 1992 and printed many times since. I had the honour of translating and publishing this book in 2002. An electronic copy is available under the "Books" section of: www.jasserauda.net

2. The hadith is authentic. Refer to Chapter 19 for more details.

3. www.unmosquedfilm.com

4. I would like to acknowledge the aboutIslam.net team for the initial translation of some of the original essays from Arabic to English. I benefited from their translation in many sections throughout this book. I would like to also note that the translation of the verses from the Quran and the narrations of hadith included in this book are mine.

5. Refer to: www.jasserauda.net

6. For a more in-depth discussion on methodology of reasoning (*ijtihad*) in the Islamic jurisprudence, refer to: Jasser Auda, *Maqāsid al-Sharīah as Philosophy of Islamic Law: A Systems Approach*, International Institute of Is-

lamic Thought, London-Washington, 2008, in addition to more recent writings.

7. For example: "[We punished] the partitioners, who have broken the Quran into unrelated shreds" (15:90–91), "Do you then believe in a part of the Book and disbelieve in the other?" (2:85), and other similar verses.

8. Abu Dawud (4291) and was verified as *sahih* (authentic) by Al-Sakhawi in *Al-Maqasid Al-Hasanah* (149) and Al-Albani in *Al-Silsilah Al-Sahihah* (599).

9. Refer to: www.corpus.quran.com for comparing translations.

10. Tafsir of Ibn Kathir, 6/67.

11. Mohammad Al-Razi, *Mukhtar Al-Sihah* (A Selection of the Correct Words), Al-Maktabah Al-'Asriyyah, Beirut, 1999/119.

12. Abul-Fadl Ibn Manzour, *Lisan Al-Arab* (The Language of Arabs), Dar Sadir, Beirut, 2003/112.

13. Bukhari, 95–6/1

14. Bukhari, chapter on Expeditions, 416/8, and Muslim, chapter on Jihad, 160/5.

15. Fat-h Al-Bary, 415/8.

16. Muslim, the chapter on ordeals, 205/8.

17. Bukhari, chapter on ablution, 300/1, and Muslim, chapter on prayer upon eclipse, 32/3.

18. Muslim, chapter on Prayer upon Eclipse, 32/3.

19. Bukhari, chapter on Prayer, 195/2 and Muslim, chapter on Masjids, 118/2.

20. Bukhari, 173/1.

21. Ahmad's *Musnad*, 511/44.

22. Bukhari, chapter on Funerals, 479/3, till the word "clamoured", and then Al-Nasa'i narrated the rest in his *Musnad*, 200/7, through the chain reported by Bukhari.

23. Bukhari, chapter on Expeditions, 416/8, and Muslim, chapter on Jihad, 160/5.

24. Muslim, chapter on Funerals, 63/3.

25. Bukhari, chapter on Prayer, 6/2; Ibn Hibban, 327/1, Al-Muwatta', 197/1, Al-Bayhaqi, 199/3, Ibn Khuzaymah, 90/3, Ibn Abu Shaybah, 156/2, Ibn Abu Shaybah, 156/2, and Ahmad on the authority of Abu Hurairah (405/15).

26. *Fat-h Al-Bary*, 34/3.

27. Bukhari 445 and Muslim 892.

28. Refer, for example, to Al-Zahabi for a detailed biography. Muhammad Al-Zahabi, *Siyar A'laam al-Nubalaa*, *Al-Risalah*, Beirut, 2001, 6/34–47.

29. Al-Tabarani's *Al-Mu'jam Al-Kabir*, 362/12 and 399/12.

30. At-Tirmidhi, 709/1, Bukhari, 305/1, Chapter: "Allowing women to frequent the mosques at night".

31. Bukhari, chapter on Prayer, 173/1; Muslim, chapter on Prayer, 328/1, and others.

32. Al-Bayhaqi 4944.

33. Ahmad 26550.

34. *Al-Mudawwanah Al-Kubra*, 106/1.

35. *Fat-h Al-Bary*, 495/2.

36. *Al-Muhalla*, 163/3.

37.   Al-Mughny, 375/2.

38.   Al-Qarafi, Al-Dhakheerah   1/153. al-Qarafi, Al-Furuq (Ma'a Hawamishih) 2/60, Burhaneddin Ibn Farhoun, Tabsirat Al-Hukkam Fi Usul Al-'Aqdiyah Wa Manahij Al-'Ahkam, ed. Jamal Mar'ashli (Beirut: Dar al-Kutub al-'ilmiyah, 1995) 2/270.

39.   Al-Qarafi, Al-Dhakheerah   1/153. al-Qarafi, Al-Furuq (Ma'a Hawamishih) 2/60.

40.   Ibn Farhoun, *Tabsirat Al-Hukkam* 2/270.

41.   *Tahrir Al-Mar'ah Fi 'Asr Ar-Risalah* (Liberating Woman in the Age of the Mission), 36/1.

42.   Al-Baihaqi, 190/3; At-Tabarani in Al-*Mu'jam Al-Kabir*, 148/25 and *Al-Ahad wal-Mathani*, 150/6.

43.   Bukhari 1190, Muslim 1394, and multiple other narrations in Bukhari, Muslim and other collections.

44.   For example, www.almunajjid.com/6433

45.   Its chain of narration is weak, so reported Al-Albani in *Al-Silsilah Al-Daeefah* 5743, Abu Nuaim in *Al-Hilya* 2/40, and others.

46.   Ibn Kathir, *Tafsir* 54/2.

47.   See for example: Ibn Hibban's *Sahih*, 6/151, Ibn Majah's *Sunan*, 1/305.

48.   See Muslim, 1/365 and Ahmad's *Musnad*, 2/299. Shu'ayb Al-Arna'ut commented on this hadith by saying that its narrators are trustworthy narrators approved by Bukhari and Muslim, even though a considerable controversy occurred regarding one of the narrators; Qatadah.

49.   Reported in Al-Daraqutni's *Sunan*, 2/196, and other nar-

rations to the same effect are reported in Abu Dawud's *Sunan*, Malik's *Muwatta'* and Ahmad's *Musnad.*

50. See Ishaq ibn Rahawayh's *Musnad*, 3/613, Ibn Hibban's *Sahih*, 6/111, and Abu Dawud's *Sunan*, 1/198. Al-Albani, commenting on Abu Dawud's narration, said that it is "authentic". And see Muslim, 1/366.

51. *Al-Um*, 1/198.

52. *Al-Muwatta*, Muhammad ibn Al-Hassan's narration, 2/58.

53. Abu Dawud's *Sunan*, 2/44.

54. Bukhari 5093, Muslim 2252.

55. Refer, for example, to the commentary of Al-Zurqani on *Al-Muwatta*, 4/216.

56. Bukhari 5776, Muslim 2224.

57. Abu Dawud 3922.

58. Al-Razi, *Al-Mahsoul*, 4/303.

59. Abu Bakr al-Maliki ibn al-Arabi, *'Aridat Al-Ahwadhi* (Cairo: Dar al-Wahy al-Mohammadi, without date) 10/264.

60. Badredin al-Zarkashi, *Al-Ijabah Li-iraad ma Is-tadrakathu Aisha ala al-Sahabah* (The Answer that Cites Aisha's Amendments to the Companions' Narrations), ed. Saeed Al-Afghani. 2nd ed., Beirut: *Al-Maktab al-Is-lami*, 1970. Jalaluddin al-Suyuti, *Ain al-Isabah fi istidrak Aisha 'ala al-sahabah* (The Right Opinions about Aisha's Amendments to the Companions' Narrations), Cairo, al-Ilm, 1409h.

61. Muslim, Chapter on Prayer, 2/32.

62. Ahmad's *Musnad*, 44/511. Al-Arna'ut said that this hadith is authentic.

63. Bukhari 5/150.

64. Bukhari (1462).

65. Bukhari (29, 3241, 5198, 6449, 6546), Muslim (2740), Tirmidhi (2602, 2603), Ahmad (2087, 3376, 7891, 5321, 19350, 19479), Ibn Hibban (7615, 7616, 7649), Bayhaqi (1345), Muwatta (445), Nasa'i (1891, 9215, 9216, 9217, 9219, 9220, 11757), Abu Dawud (872, 2882), Al-Bazzar (5340), Jami Muammar Ibn Rashid (20610, 20611), and Tabarani (2485, 12765, 12766, 12767).

66. Quran 9:100, 48:25, 48:29, 58:22, and others.

67. Ibn Hibban (7649).

68. See Wafa' Al-Wafa Bi-Akhbar Dar Al-Mustafa, 1/75–249.

69. Bukhari, chapter on Funerals, 3/479, till the word "clamoured", and then Al-Nasa'i narrated the rest, 7/200, through the chain reported by Bukhari.

70. Muslim, the chapter on ordeals, 8/205.

71. Muslim, the chapter on Friday, 3/13.

72. Bukhari, the chapter on Adhan 2/388, Muslim, The Prayer Chapter 2/40.

73. Muslim, The Virtues Chapter 4/1795 .

74. Bukhari, The Merits 7/244. Muslim, Companions' Merits, 7/144

75. Muslim, chapter on Eclipse, 3/32.

76. See Ibn Sa'd's *At-Tabaqat Al-Kubra*, 3/609, and Wafa'

Al-Wafa Bi-Akhbar Dar Al-Mustafa, 1/75–249.

77. Abu Dawud's *Sunan*, 1/348. Ibn Hazm referenced it in *Al-Muhalla*, 3/131 and Ibn 'Abdul Bar in *At-Tamhid*, 23/397. It is also referenced by At-Tabarani in *Al-Awsat*, 1018, and Bukhari in *At-Tarikh Al-Kabir*, 1/60, on the authority of Omar who said, "Men! Do not enter the mosque through the women's entrance".

78. Bukhari 1/255

79. Ibn Hibban 6/221

80. Bukhari 1/109

81. Bukhari 1/143

82. As reported from Anas in Az-Zawa'id by Abu Ya'la Al-Mawsili. A similar report is narrated in Bukhari and Muslim in the above two references.

83. Bukhari, chapter on Funerals, 479/3, till the word "clamoured", and then An-Nasa'i narrated the rest in his *Musnad*, 200/7, through the chain reported by Bukhari.

84. See Malik's *Al-Muwatta*, 24/1, and Ahmad's *Musnad*, 103/2, and the report includes "And they would start it (ablution) together". See also An-Nasa'i's *Sunan*, chapter on purification, section on men and women performing ablution together, 57/1, and Ibn Khuzaymah's *Sahih*, 63/1.

85. *Musannaf*, Abu Shaybah, 319/6.as

86. *Jami Bayan Al-'Ilm Wa Fadlihi*, 375/1.

87. *Al-Mu'jam Al-Awsat*, 158/6. It was also narrated by An-Nasa'i from Anas, 400/2.

88. *Al-Mu'jam Al-Kabir*, 173/24.

89. Ibn Abu Shaybah's *Musannaf*, 391/4.

90. Bukhari, chapter on Expeditions, 416/8, and Muslim, chapter on Jihad, 160/5.

91. Fat-h Al-Bary, 415/8.

92. Ibn Kathir's *Musnad Al-Farouq*, 573/2, and Abu Ya'la's *Az-Zawa'id*, 335/2.

93. Al-Hakim stated that "this Hadith is of an authentic chain of narration, though Bukhari and Muslim did not reference it." See also Ibn Khuzaymah's *Sahih*, 818/2, and Ibn Hibban's *Sahih*, 2/126.

94. *Sharh Ma'ani Al-Athar*, 3/14. It is also recorded in *Al-Mustadrak*, 2/179, and Al-Hakim said, "This hadith is authentic according to the criterion set by Ash-Shaykhayn (Bukhari and Muslim), though they did not reference it." It is also reported in other reference books.

95. Nasa'i 2642, Ahmad 2266, Ibn Hazm's *Muhallah* 2/248.

96. Bukhari, Chapter on Prayer, 2/195, and Muslim, Chapter on Mosques, 2/118.

97. Al-Hakim's *Al-Mustdrak 'ala al-Sahihin*, 2/430. Al-Hakim said that this hadith has an authentic chain of reporters though it is not narrated by Bukhari or Muslim.

98. Muslim, Chapter on Prayer, 2/31 and Ibn Khuzaimah's *Sahih*, 3/90..

99. Muslim, 1/328, and Abu Na'eem's *Al-Musnad al-Mustakhraj 'ala Sahih Muslim* 2/65 and other sources.

100. Abu Dawud 4/79.

101. Ibn Hazm, *Al-Muhalla, Kitab al-Salah*, Hadith 427.

102. Muslim 505.

103. Ibn Khuzaimah 1229, Ibn Majah 762, Nasa'i 797.

104. Ibn Hibban 5308.

105. Tabarani 3765, Bayhaqi 12501.

106. Al-Hakim's *Al-Mustadrak 'Ala As-Sahihayn,* the author states, "it is authentic according to the criterion set by Ash-Shaykhayn, though they did not report it" (1/425), Abu Dawud's *Sunan,* 2/295, Abu Shaybah's *Musannaf,* 2/109, and Ash-Shafi'i's *Musnad,* 1/61.

107. *Subul As-Salam,* 2/58.

108. Bukhari, 131/1.

109. Bukhari, 66/3.

110. Ibn Al-Qayyim, *Zad al-Ma'ad,* 550-552.

111. Ibn Kathir, *Tafsir* 54/2.

112. *Fiqh At-Taharah,* 100.

113. Bukhari, *At-Tarikh Al-Kabir,* 786/1, Al-Bayhaqui, *Sunan,* 620/2, and Abu Dawud, *Sunan,* 60/1.

114. Musnad Ishaq Ibn Rahaweeh 1783, and it is at the rank of hasan (good).

115. Bukhari, *Sahih,* 95-6/1.

116. *Al-Muhalla,* 776–7/1.

117. *Majmu' Al-Fatawa,* 179/26.

118. *I'lam Al-Muwaqqi'in,* 25/3.

119. Bukhari 3/37; and Muslim 2/798. The report quoted here is Muslim's version.

120. Bukhari, chapter on Expeditions, 416/8, and Muslim, chapter on Jihad, 160/5.

121. *Fathul Bary*, 415/8.

122. Abu Shaybah's *Musannaf*, 319/6.as

123. Bukhari 445 and Muslim 892.

124. Bukhari (1462).

125. Bukhari, chapter on Expeditions, 416/8, and Muslim, chapter on Jihad, 160/5.

126. Ibn Khuzaimah 1229, Ibn Majah 762, Nasa'i 797.

127. Bukhari, chapter on fasting 5/177

128. Editor's note: according to scholars, this question means, "Is the real purpose of pitching these tents devotion and worship or is it only a matter of wives' rivalry and competition?"

129. Bukhari, chapter on women i'tikaf, 3/48–49.

130. Bukhari (3/49), chapter on houses of the Prophet's wives, Muslim (4/1712); Al-Baihaqi in *As-Sunan Al-Kubra* (4/529); chapter on woman's visiting her husband in i'tikaf; Ibn Khuzaimah (3/349) in his *Sahih*, Chapter on concession (rukhsah) for woman to visit her husband in i'tikaf; Ibn Hibban in his *Sahih*, chapter on permissibility of woman's visiting her husband in i'tikaf during night; and others.

131. *Dawr al-Mar'ah fi khidmat al-Hadith fil Qurun ath-ala-thah al-awla* (Women's Role in Serving Hadith During the First Three Decades), Amala Qurdash bint al-Husain, Al-Ummah Book, Ministry of Awqaf and Islamic Affairs, Researches and Studies Center, Qatar, Vol. 70, 1999.

132. Mohammad Akram Nadwi, *Al-Muhaddithat: The Wom-*

en Scholars in Islam (Oxford: Interface Publications, 2007).

133. *Al-Muhaddithat*/138.

134. Mohammad Al-Azimabadi, *Awn al-Ma'bud*, Beirut: Dar al-Fikr, 1995/226.

135. Al-Hakim, *Al-ustadrak 'ala As-Sahihain*, 1/320.

136. Al-Moghni 3/37.

137. Ibn Majah, *Sunan*, 2/183 and 1/343.

138. Ibn Abi Shaibah's Musanaf 1/430.

139. Al-Muwatta (Muhammad ibn Al-Hasan's narration) 2/58. It is also reported by At-Tabarani and Abdur-Razzaq.

140. Abdur-Razzaq's Musannaf 3/149.

141. Abu Dawud's *Sunan* 1/442 591.

142. Ibn Saad, *Kitab al-Tabaqat al-Kabir*, 8/335.

143. *Nasb Ar-Rayah* 2/32.

144. Ibn Khuzaimah 2/810.

145. Al-Badr Al-Muneer 4/392.

146. Subul As-Salam 2/35.

147. Naqd Maratib al-Ijma' 290.

148. Al-Qawa'id An-Nuraniyah 1/120.

149. *Al-Moghni fi Fiqh Al-Imam Ahmad ibn Hanbal Ash-Shaibani* 2/34.

150. Ibn Taymiyyah, *Majmu' Al-Fatawa*, Medina: Majma' Fahd, 1995, 22/249.

151. *Al-Mustdarak 'ala As-Sahihain* 1/320. It is also reported

by Al-Baihaqi 1/600, Ibn Abi Shaibah 1/202 and others.

152. Nasb Al-Rayah 2/32.

153. Bukhari 4425, and Nasa'i 8/227 under the chapter titled: "Forbidding the rulership of women".

154. Al-Zahabi, *Siyar A'lam al-Nubala*, Beirut: *Al-Risala*, 2001, 3/5.